MY FAVOU

IPSWICH ⌐vvIN

edited by Susan Gardiner

electric blue publishing

First published 2017 by Electric Blue Publishing, Stowmarket, Suffolk, IP14 5AE.

www.electric-blue.co.uk

ISBN 978-0-9955396-4-8 (paperback)

Contents

Introduction

Asking a number of very different Ipswich Town fans to write about their "favourite game" might have produced a set of predictable, even obvious, results. Ipswich supporters are famous for their tendency to live in the past, to look backwards towards a time when their team was one of the most famous in Europe, or when they had given not one, but two, brilliant managers to the national side, Sir Alf Ramsey and Sir Bobby Robson. The twenty-first century has not been kind to Ipswich Town - nor to a large number of similar football sides, outside the manufactured elite of the top six or seven clubs in the Premier League. It's extremely difficult for any club that is not part of a huge, global business to garner the resources to build the massive stadia, or to buy - and keep happy - the multimillion pound "stars" of the game. So it might have been excusable for Ipswich Town supporters to have chosen to dwell in the halcyon Robson (or even Ramsey) days but - despite the fact that some of the contributors to this book can remember at least the time when Bobby Robson was manager - they have chosen, if not more recent matches, certainly very different games to what might have been the obvious choices, as their favourites. For example, the earliest game in this collection was one that took place between Ipswich and Chelmsford City in the third round of the FA Cup in 1973. Similarly, another choice from the Robson era, is not, as might be expected, the UEFA Cup finals of 1981, or even the match when Town beat Arsenal to win the FA Cup in 1978, but a match in the earlier rounds of the Cup, against Millwall the same season when a near-riot took place at the Old Den.

First games, games with friends or family, loved ones, seem to be the real favourites. One contributor was lucky enough to find her first ever match was one which boasted a team that any Ipswich fan, then or now, would relish, as arguably (with the exception of a missing Kevin Beattie) the best, the most accomplished footballing side Portman Road ever saw: Cooper, Burley, Mills, Thijssen, Osman, Butcher, Wark, Mühren, Mariner, Brazil and Gates.

Another predictable choice would be one of the so-called "Old Farm" derby games, matches played against our chief and abiding enemies in Norfolk, but although this collection includes one supreme example of that genre, matches against our traditional rivals don't seem to make the grade as the great footballing spectacles that they perhaps should be. In fact, it's interesting that our other great rivalry with the "Norwich of the North," Sheffield United features twice in this book.

Away trips are also surprisingly near-absent from this selection, although there are intrepid trips to Moscow and Foggia, which is probably as obscure a town to English fans as Ipswich is to most Italians. The nights under the lights at Portman Road appear to be particularly strong in the memory, ranging from the spurious glamour of playing the stars of Internazionale to what has become a perennial favourite, the play-off match. There were probably more play-off games that could have been recounted here - I remember a particularly passionate encounter (which, annoyingly, we lost) against West Ham at Portman Road and I don't think there will be many who demur from the view that the very apotheosis of those matches (or of any game for the genuine fan) would be the 5-3 victory over Bolton Wanderers in the semi-final play-off match in 2000. It has been written about several times, and no doubt, there will be more about this remarkable match, its atmosphere of crackling electricity, the ultimate in all the aspects of the game that keep us addicted: passion, sporting prowess and sheer, unadulterated craziness.

Alongside these we have some odd treats: the last home game of the season against Crewe, and a quite recent game at Watford by our youngest contributor. It is clearly not our greatest victories and achievements as a football club that stay most deeply in our hearts and minds, but other things, less tangible than silverware but perhaps more valuable in the end: love, family, friendship and sport.

ONE

Ipswich Town 2 Norwich City 1
Sunday, 14 April 1996
Portman Road

Sunday April 14th 1996. I remember this day as if it was yesterday. I leapt out of bed before my Sonic the Hedgehog alarm clock had time to go off and I raced down the stairs three at a time. I didn't care that it was early Sunday morning, because today's date was far more significant; it was my birthday! I rushed into the lounge, faster than one of Ipswich right-back Gus Uhlenbeek's infamous runs, desperate to see what presents would be nestled around the coffee table. I hurriedly unwrapped the blue and white wrapping paper and was elated to receive some brilliant gifts, including Ipswich's stylish 1995/96 replica away kit - the classic Core-designed bottle green jersey with maroon sleeves. Amongst my other gifts was the latest ITFC annual, the new club video and a pair of Nike Air Jordan XI trainers.

However, all these presents were eclipsed by what was handed to me next. I carefully opened the envelope and inside I found tickets for the Ipswich Players' Lounge that had been given to me by club captain, Tony Mowbray. I ran around the room chanting "Georgie Burley's Blue and White Army," whilst waving the tickets above my head. I was lucky enough to get to know Tony Mowbray after hanging around for autographs at the end of home games. Little did I know that a friend had mentioned it to the Ipswich captain that my birthday was coming up and the man from Saltburn secretly passed on the tickets as a gift. Not only was I going to be mixing with some of my footballing idols, in particular the Argentinian, Mauricio Taricco, I was also hoping I would be in the company of a few disappointed players from our arch-rivals Norwich City. Despite pestering to leave for the game right away, I was told it was only 6:45am and that I had to wait until noon before we set off for the 3pm kick-off at Portman Road.

Later, as we travelled by car to the game I was sat in the back seat devouring my own body weight in Fruit Salad Black Jack sweets. As we parked up I was told to stop eating the sweets as I'd make myself sick. "But it's my birthday," I whined. "But you're twenty-five today Seán, not six!" It was clear to me that I wasn't excited because I was celebrating my twenty-fifth year on Planet Earth, it was because Ipswich were playing that team from up the A140 and I was lucky enough to have tickets to the Players' Lounge afterwards.

Back in the early 1990s Sunday kick-offs were still in their infancy and this was the first time that Ipswich had met the Canaries at Portman Road on the Sabbath. The game had been moved back a day to accommodate ITV's live coverage. Fortunately, the independent broadcaster hadn't adopted Sky Sports' approach of fireworks and cheerleaders as pre-match entertainment, so there was time for a few pints of Guinness in the Black Horse pub before heading towards Portman Road. As I walked to the ground I could already hear singing and chanting from both sets of fans and the butterflies in my stomach began to stretch their wings. Despite this I was feeling optimistic and I headed to the Ladbroke's hut underneath the Churchman's Stand to place a bet on Ipswich to win the game 4-2. I fancied Ipswich's "M&M" strike force, Ian Marshall and Alex Mathie, to continue their rich vein of form in front of goal - with six games left of the season, Marshall and Mathie were on seventeen and sixteen goals respectively. They say that old habits die hard and still to this day I have a small gamble on a 4-2 Town win every game.

Ipswich went in to the Norwich game off back-to-back defeats. The previous weekend Town had lost 2-1 at home to Reading on Easter Saturday and then the Blues failed to rise again on Easter Monday losing 3-1 away to Grimsby. That game at Blundell Park was one that's best to forget. Central defender Tony Vaughan was sent off for a straight red in the thirty-sixth minute, the referee rightly adjudging Vaughan to be the last defender as he hauled down former Ipswich striker Neil Woods. In the second half Grimsby striker Clive Mendonca took full advantage of the extra man by scoring a hat-trick for The Mariners.

Against Norwich, Ipswich took to the pitch in what is quite possibly their worst ever home shirt. You know the one; the drip-dried blue fading to white monstrosity sponsored by local brewer, Greene King. The only benefit that I could see to having such a horrendous shirt was that a referee could easily spot if a Town player's shirt was being tugged out of his shorts by their opponents. Ipswich manager George Burley and his Norwich counterpart Gary Megson shook hands before the Old Farm Derby kicked off. Burley no doubt reminding the Norwich boss that it was a little over two years since Megson himself became an instant Portman Road hero, when the Norwich defender scored an own goal (a bullet header) to secure all three points for Town in a 2-1 win.

The game started off in a lively fashion with Ipswich looking to return to the top six following the previous day's results. At the midpoint of the first half a through-ball to Ian Marshall saw the ungainly striker volley Town into the lead from the edge of the box. Town took this lead into the half-time interval. Norwich, sitting in fifteenth place, brought on substitute Jamie Cureton in the second half and the Bristol-born striker soon equalised for the Canaries. John Wark had replaced Tony Vaughan in the starting line-up for the Scotsman's first start in eight matches and it was Wark's uncharacteristic slip that allowed Cureton to equalise. A hopeful ball from Darren Eadie wrong-footed Wark and once the Norwich striker received the ball he hammered it past keeper Richard Wright into the top left corner. Cureton, who had dyed his hair green for the occasion, then ran off towards the North Stand with a celebration that could only be described as "stupid man repeatedly hitting green coloured bonce with hand."

With five minutes left on the stadium clock the East Anglian Derby looked to be heading towards its first draw in thirteen years. Both sets of fans were probably considering taking the draw as it would make it easier heading into work the next day knowing your team hadn't lost the "big" game. Suddenly the Ipswich players broke down a Norwich move and chased the ball down into the middle of the Norwich half, where the ball found its way to the feet of Robert Ullathorne. The Norwich full back casually rolled the ball back to Bryan Gunn and the Scottish keeper, under minimal pressure from James Scowcroft, looked to clear the ball up the Portman Road pitch. However, Gunn's kick only contacted with thin air as the ball hit a divot, went over his swinging limb and rolled slowly in to the back of the goal. Portman Road erupted in to a cacophony of cheers and laughter. In the penalty area, Bryan Gunn was crestfallen on one knee and the hapless Ullathorne was on the verge of tears. It took a few seconds for all of this to sink in with me, had I just witnessed another comedy own goal scored by Norwich at Portman Road? Euphoria quickly kicked in and I joined in with the Ipswich fans's chant of "Let's all do a Gunny!" whilst hilariously kicking our right legs into the air. Amongst all of this, a section of Ipswich fans ran out on to the pitch and there was a short delay as the stewards regained control. Ipswich controlled the last few minutes of the game and the man in black, Jim Rushton, blew his whistle to signal the end of the encounter. It was an incredible twenty-second home win of the season for the Super

Blues.

The referee hadn't finished blowing into his whistle before the Ipswich Town fans spilled out on to the pitch from all stands. It is at this point where I should confess that I got a little bit carried away with the occasion and I too ventured on to the Portman Road turf. It was the second time I had found myself on the playing surface within the last twelve months. The previous occasion was at the end of the season before, when Ipswich fans chaired off local lad, Richard Wright, after his Premier League debut.

As I joined my fellow Town fans on the pitch, I noticed we were all basically leaping about with the biggest grins on our faces. I then remembered I had my Players' Lounge tickets in my pocket and turned around to go back into the Churchman's Stand. As I turned around I came face to face with the Norwich number one. He was easy to spot in his multi-coloured keeper's jersey. Now I'm not sure what the protocol is for this type of encounter, but I believed I uttered the words "Well played Bryan!" Gunn responded to my possibly sarcastic comment by taking off his right glove and offering to shake my hand. I must admit it was at this point that I felt a bit bad, well for a second anyway, and I went to accept the Scot's handshake. As our hands were about to touch I felt my collar being grabbed and both my arms were forced behind my back. I looked over my shoulder to see that I was being ushered off the pitch by two stewards. I suggested that they were being a bit unjust considering there were still hundreds of Ipswich fans running around the pitch. My protests fell on deaf ears.

After spending the afternoon watching our boys in blue, I soon found myself standing next to boys in blue of a different kind. As I stood in a holding area I gave an embarrassed smile towards the policemen, they returned my look with a grimace and quickly my gaze fixed on my new Nike trainers. One of the police officers asked me what I had done to find myself standing in the holding area. I quickly told him that today was my birthday, hoping it would help my case, and that I went on the pitch to offer my commiserations to Bryan Gunn, which was almost the truth, I told myself. The policeman replied, "Wait, you've been brought here for that? Look up there," he pointed towards the Norwich fans who were currently dismantling the Cobbold Stand seat by seat. The policeman looked at me, almost with pity and said, "As it is your birthday, why don't you just p... ...!" I don't think he'd got to the last two words of that sentence before I turned heel and hurried myself back to the stand.

I made my way to the entrance that leads to the Players' Lounge and offered my complimentary tickets to the steward. Fortunately for me it was a different steward to those who escorted me off the pitch earlier. After a few flights of the Pioneer Stand's concrete steps, I opened the door into the Players's Lounge. I sat there nervously waiting for the door to open to see which Town players would come and celebrate the game. Soon enough the players came in, including an overjoyed Ian Marshall. Finally, Tony Mowbray entered the room and the big centre-half came over and wished me a happy birthday and asked if I could have dreamt of a birthday gift like the game I had just witnessed. Later as I mixed with the Town players, the door swung open and in walked Bryan Gunn. I hadn't even considered that "Gunny" would show his face, I felt he would have wanted to get on the team coach as soon as possible. Mind you I never considered him becoming the Sheriff of Norwich either! I spent the next ten minutes trying to avoid the Norwich keeper by hiding behind my pint glass and a potted plant. I breathed a huge sigh of relief as Gunn wished good luck to the remaining Town players and headed back out the door.

Later that evening I returned home and received a phone call from my Mum. She asked me about the game and wanted to know how I got on in the Players' Lounge. We laughed about Bryan Gunn's air-kick and she told me that the local *Evening Star* newspaper was producing a celebratory badge to mark the occasion. My Mother then enquired if I went on to the pitch at the end of the game. I told my Mum that I had decided to stay in the stand to celebrate at the end to allow me to head off to the Players' Lounge as soon as the last Town player headed down the tunnel. Well, I know. Judge me as you will.

The next day I ensured I was home from work in time to watch the goals on the local Anglia news programme. I unwrapped a new JVC videotape and clicked record on my VCR as yesterday's highlights began. I've no idea if I laughed more at Gunn's comical effort or Ullathorne's blubbing face. My laughter soon disappeared as the coverage moved on to the pitch invasion at the end and the camera focussed on my bemused face as I was being escorted off the pitch. Within twenty seconds my phone started to ring. "Hello," I said nervously as I picked up the handset. The voice on the other end of the phone was that of my Mum. She had also been watching the sports news and it was clear she was not happy.

The moral to this story is, *never ever lie to your Mum.*

Seán Salter

7

Ipswich Town 2 Norwich City 1
Division One 1995/96
Attendance: 20,355
Referee: Jim Rushton

IPSWICH TOWN

Manager: George Burley

Team: Richard Wright, Gus Uhlenbeek, Mauricio
Taricco, Mick Stockwell, John Wark, Geraint Williams, Paul
Mason, Steve Sedgley, James Scowcroft, Ian Marshall, Simon
Milton (Subs: Tony Vaughan, Richie Appleby)

Goals: Marshall (23)
        Ullathorne (o.g. 86)

NORWICH CITY

Manager: Gary Megson

Team: Bryan Gunn, Carl Bradshaw, Rob
Ullathorne, Ian Crook, John Polston, Rob Newman, Neil
Adams, Robert Fleck, Ade Akinbiyi, Mike Milligan, Darren
Eadie (Subs: Spencer Prior, Andy Johnson, Jamie Cureton)

Goals: Cureton (62)

TWO

Ipswich Town 3 Sheffield United 2
Saturday, 8 February 2003
Portman Road

"It's going to be a good 'un today," I optimistically announced as I reached my seat in the North Stand. "Everyone's going to be up for it; it's going to be one of them."

Who would doubt me as I had correctly predicted the score a few months ago. The fact that approximately 216 predictions had been wrong since then was immaterial. Details! No this one was different. It wasn't so much the result I was predicting here, but that the match would be fierce, well contested and full of vigour.

There were a few reasons for this. The first being our history with Sheffield United. They'd knocked us out of the play-offs a few years ago in an agitated match that saw Mauricio Tarrico giving it some. Those things stuck. Then there was Neil Warnock, the then manager of the Blades. On the list of "people we love to hate," he has a strong polling. For what it's worth, I quite like him. However it was inevitable that the crowd would give him stick. These two issues would create an atmosphere - and not the kind Russ Abbott sang about.

Perhaps more importantly, this was the first game at Portman Road following the sad death of Dale Roberts. Roberts had been an instrumental figure in Town's return to the Premier League. He and the then manager, George Burley, had implemented superb passing football at Portman Road. The kind of football that gained us plaudits in the top tier. We had a season in the sun where we shone, beating some of the better teams in the Premier League and finishing fifth. The scalps of Liverpool, Leeds United (when they were good - ask your mum or dad, kids), Newcastle (see Leeds) and Tottenham Hotspur were amongst those taken. Marcus Stewart was a household name, despite playing for Ipswich! It was Roy of the Rovers stuff.

The following season was gloomy. It is true we did not have the best of luck, but something was missing. We did not play so well, we scored less, we conceded more. Roberts had sadly become ill and less involved with the coaching at the club. Town were relegated to whatever Division Two was then called (at the time of writing, it's the Championship - I think). We were tipped for a swift return to the Premier League. Alas the season started badly. Following poor results, Burley was sacked.

A few months later, Roberts sadly passed away. This was the end of an era. The dream was over. A minute's silence was to be held. Often these result in the crowd being fired up afterwards. Along with the rivalry, such atmospheres bring everyone to their feet. Rob Chandler (the PA man) introduced the silence with the two teams standing on the halfway circle. I can't quite recall the exact point or words, but something during his eulogy caused all fans to applaud in respect. Sheffield United fans joined in. There was something in particular about this introduction, perhaps about Roberts himself, but there was a feeling of loss and of pride and the unity that football provides. It was sad, yet warming. The minute's silence was immaculately observed by both sets of fans. The referee's whistle indicated the minute was up and was met with an emotional roar from all four stands at Portman Road. As tears were mopped and appreciative nods made towards the away end, all indicated they wanted a game to match that respect. As players took their position, bigger cheers than normal greeted them. They too looked impassioned by the showing of respect. Of course these things rarely go to plan. There is no scriptwriter in football, apart from for Roy of the Rovers. This was not Roy of the Rovers but Ipswich Town playing Sheffield United. After twenty minutes, Pablo Couñago was sent off. Perhaps it's a contractual thing with Latin footballers wearing an Ipswich Town shirt, especially against Sheffield United. Peter Ndlovu then showed that he is not sixty-seven years old as previously thought by skipping through the Town defence Maradona style.

"We'll still give it away," I thought only to see him deliver a fine shot past Andy Marshall and into the onion bag.

"I knew he'd do that!" I lied.

The Sheffield United fans celebrated to the tune of *Tom Hark*. It was annoying. "Bollocks" was the constructive word bandied about at half time. United were a good team and it was a good match, but none amongst us could see us overcoming a goal deficit with one player less. And a particularly good player at that. As someone said, coming back from one goal down with a man less is possible. The scriptwriter was clearly employed by Sheffield

United as the half time scores were announced. Norwich City (our local rivals) were beating Sheffield Wednesday. Our disappointment was beaten by Sheffield United's delight. This was not our day. Losing when your rival team wins is up there with standing on a plug or a paper cut when it comes to painful experience. Anyone who disagrees is a liar or a robot. Town lined up in the second half with a 3-3-3 formation. Joe Royle made substitutions and Marcus Bent became the target/hold up man spearheading the attack. Darrens Ambrose and Bent (town's stars of the future) playing wide off him. This was ambitious on behalf of Royle. Bloody dangerous too, but what the hell, we were going for it. Maybe...

From the off, the attacks were again greeted with roars. This half, Town were attacking the North Stand (the noisiest stand at Portman Road). Even though victory seemed unlikely, we wanted something out of this. Sheffield United, Neil Warnock, Dale Roberts and now the sense of injustice following Couñago's red card prevailed. The noise went up to eleven. Eleven out of ten, that is, not one hundred. We're clear?

It was clear Paddy Kenny's goal was under threat. Kenny was the quintessential Neil Warnock goalkeeper. I guess you could interpret that as saying he had character. He also received plenty of abuse with chants of "You Fat Bastard!" This, despite him not being fat and the average chanter of this being above average weight.

"I can sense a goal!" Someone announced with a smile. They were right, as Dean Windass scored from outside the box to put the Blades two-nil up. Once again, their fans celebrated with *Tom flippin' Hark*. They were loud with their repetition of this to our silence. The tune hung in the air, depressingly so.

This was clearly unfair. We'd had our hopes raised, only to have them dashed within five minutes of the game restarting. And since when did Windass become so good at shooting? It was bad enough that Ndlovu had become the new Eric Gates. Pah, football. Hate it.

But then it happened. Darren Bent picked up Jermaine Wright's fine pass to put the ball past Paddy Kenny and reduce the deficit to 2-1. We had a goal to celebrate. Bent picked the ball out of the net, showing his intention and determination to take the game to United. Looks were exchanged in the North Stand between optimists and pessimists of "Could we? It's possible." But nobody dared to say it. But the volume was now up to 11.2!

The attacks came at both ends. With Town now only having three in midfield, the Blades were able to have more freedom. This was an end to end match. No, not all of the football was pretty. Marcus Bent playing the game of his life in winning every ball passed/hoofed/thrown in his direction. Boy was he good. The Darrens were buzzing off and around him, unsettling the Sheffield United defence. A defence that was brutal. Brilliant, but brutal.

Each contest that town won, were it Holland or Miller winning the ball, Marcus Bent outjumping and outmuscling a defender or a Darren scaring the shit out of a seasoned defender, the crowd roared louder and louder. The atmosphere building and building. This was added to by the screams and despair as the Blades attacked and came close. Tension was firmly present too, for both us and the Sheffield United fans. They were continuing to roar on their team. I was impressed with them. They kept a chant going for what seemed like twenty minutes, a wall of noise to back their players. This in turn seemed to make us louder.

As we went close, someone said "If we get an equaliser, this place will go off!" Minutes later, this proved to be correct. It was scrappy and followed an almighty long ball, but Ambrose headed past the hapless Kenny to equalise. And that was it. Pande-fuckin-monium.

Celebrations were amazing as we cheered and saluted the team. It wasn't so much that hugs were exchanged but that everyone just grabbed one another (not in a Trump way, might I add). Scenes (as the kids would say - I think?). Some appeared to end up in a row different to where they had been moments before.

Two all. Two all having been two-nil down. This was the opposite to the usual ITFC way. This was *us* turning the tables. And with being a man down. We couldn't, could we? Could we get a winner? What followed may not have been in the purists' book of football, but it was beautiful nonetheless. Both sides were giving it their all and matched by the fans from both sides. Attacks came and went at both ends. We knew we could win. We knew we could lose. Our pride was high having came back; hopeful, yet scared.

United went on the attack and sent a low shot that whilst fizzing along, appeared to take forever, slow motion stuff. We all knew it was goalbound from the moment he struck it and as it skidded along the ground. A feeling of despair gripped, someone cried "Oh no!" until it just whispered wide of the goal. I'm not sure what was louder; the "oohs" from the Blades or the relief from Town. Of course we all did that "aahhh" thing to mock our opposing fans, making out that we were never worried. We were soon back underway and returned with the attacks. And then the most amazing moment, or should I say most amazing minutes, of my time supporting Ipswich Town happened.

Ambrose crossed, it missed Marcus Bent, but there was Darren Bent to nod the ball in! Goal! Three-Two!

If the celebrations had been passionate for the equaliser, this was a few notches higher. It was mayhem, mayhem in a good way. I don't think I've ever been happier at a football ground. Everyone was on Cloud Nine and the love for the players was immense. We had found ourselves some heroes. Should I mention Roy of the Rovers again? Tom Hark was then played as an ironic insult to the Blades by Rob Chandler. The town fans joined in celebration and mockery. And then the final whistle. Joy, relief, incredulous, orgasmic screams and the whole of ITFC applauded off the pitch as though they were the ones who had won the League, the FA Cup and UEFA Cup. There was pride here. Amazing passion. We were thoroughly entertained.

PA man Chandler then announced "That was for you, Dale." Perfect. I might have gotten something in my eye. Quite a few people appeared to have.

Handshakes and warm smiles were shared throughout. I felt giddy, smiling like something that smiles a lot. Friendships were made on the back of the result and the celebrations. I will always be grateful to have witnessed that game. It was a fitting memorial for Dale Roberts. It gave me respect for the Sheffield United fans due to their noise throughout the game and their silence for Dale. Warnock, gracious in defeat, rocketed in my heart. But that day, I could not have loved Ipswich Town FC, players, supporters and staff, more.

I'm not sure if it was a case of Ipswich being back or if it was a new version, but it felt good. There was hope for the future, it looked bright. The smile was unlikely to leave for months. Two days later, Ipswich Town announced they had gone into administration, or a version of. The smile disappeared. Ambrose was sold for a song. Brutal and definitely not beautiful.

Stuart Hellingsworth

Ipswich Town 3 Sheffield United 2
Division One 2002/03
Attendance: 26,151
Referee: Richard Beeby

IPSWICH TOWN

Manager: Joe Royle

Team: Andy Marshall, Fabian Wilnis, Thomas Gaardsoe, Hermann Hreiðarsson, Chris Makin, Matt Holland, Jim Magilton, Tommy Miller, Pablo Couñago, Darren Bent, Darren Ambrose. (Subs: Jermaine Wright, Marcus Bent)

Goals: D. Bent (57, 88)
Ambrose (78)

SHEFFIELD UNITED

Manager: Neil Warnock

Team: Paddy Kenny, Phil Jagielka, Shsun Murphy, Robert Page, Wayne Quinn, Peter Ndlovu, Michael Brown, Stuart McCall, Michael Tonge, Dean Windass, Steve Kabba (Subs: Richard Edghill, Wayne Allison, Tommy Mooney).

Goals: Ndlovu (45)
Windass (50)

THREE

Ipswich Town 4 Everton 0
Saturday, 30 August 1980
Portman Road

I've often questioned my allegiance to Ipswich Town. More recently this has likely been triggered by incredulity at the regular and often time-consuming, will-sapping tube/bus/train trek to Suffolk through years of mid-table mediocrity and lack of investment in the squad, but previously I've been questioned as a Wigan born, Leeds raised fan as to how the link was created. The common (read: incorrect and patronising) assumption is that I must have been coerced into life as a card-carrying football supporter through a boyfriend or other male acquaintance. However I can confirm that no males were harmed, or otherwise deeply involved, in the making of this particular fan.

In some ways, I feel like I should be facing a Mrs Merton-esque question in the style of her infamous probe to Debbie Magee: "What drew you to the much lauded, talent packed Ipswich team managed by Bobby Robson in the 1970s?" but in fact, the flow chart of decision making which led me to Ipswich was rather more logical, based on a series of questions which started from "Do you accept that supporting Leeds United is beyond the pale?" through "Will you rule out all London clubs?" and onwards, whittling down to an eventual shortlist of one and only one: ITFC.

Football fandom was not exactly rife in my family: Dad occasionally expressed an interest in an Arsenal result, otherwise we followed a seasonal sporting diet of rugby league, cricket and Wimbledon, all of which we absorbed through radio, TV or news reports rather than watching live games. A move to Leeds in the era of Don Revie's squad of hard men, witnessing the regular lockdown of the city centre on match days to allow throughput

of their rabid fans did not encourage a love of the game, so it was something
of a surprise to come across a couple of new friends in my early teens
who were keen supporters of Liverpool and Manchester United. Bonding
through a mutual dislike of our local team, with their encouragement I
nurtured an initial interest in following the sport in general, via *Final Score*
and *Match of the Day*, gradually coming to the realisation that extended life
as a neutral fan made no sense, I needed *my* team. And so to my logical
selection flowchart that led inexorably to the choice that still rules much of
my year.

My first season as a Town fan was in 1977/78 and with the FA Cup
win at the end of the year, I felt sure that a life of endless silverware and
glory lay ahead. It's difficult to say whether my early enthusiasm for the
club would have waned had we not had such a memorable victory, but at
the time, it appeared that I had picked not only logically, but wisely, and for
the next couple of seasons my support never wavered. My teenage diaries,
which previously were mainly about food, films and falling outs, begin to
mention score lines, scorers and even the odd comment as to whether we
were robbed, or deserved victors. Gradually it must have dawned on all of
us that this was an interest which was not going to go away and so, in August
1980, having returned from a trip to Holland, during which I received my O
level results, I record in my diary that there were a number of presents and
congratulations cards waiting for me, but that by far the best of these was
the news that my dad was going to take me to Portman Road for not only my
first trip to see Ipswich Town, but my first live game of football.

Maybe the trek from Yorkshire to Essex to stay with friends ahead of the
game should have been taken as a portent for a future regular round trip of
160 miles; mum has said on more than one occasion 'I wonder if we'd have
let you go to Portman Road for that game if we knew the impact it would
have on you?" (I don't quite buy this however, as mum was also the one
who encouraged me to follow the team through Russia, Italy and the Czech
Republic on their short lived European resurgence in 2001/2 and 2002/3).
Whatever else, that first game instantly created a love of live sport which
has never dwindled, I can get easily bored watching televised sport, but even
a relatively uneventful 0-0 can still keep me happily entertained, as can live
cricket, rugby, sumo, golf, tennis - pretty much anything other than motor
sports.

Looking back, what I remember the most of that day is not so much the
game itself but the sheer thrill of seeing players who until then had been
only tiny figures on a TV screen running out onto the pitch in front of me.
It's still a highlight of the year, that moment when the players emerge from

the tunnel at Portman Road for the first game of the season. Then again, it's the hope that kills you.

The game for me was less about the details of the team set up, or any individual brilliance of a particular attacking or defensive move, although there was plenty of that in evidence in that fabulous group of players, but more about the whole experience: live action, the noise and excitement of the crowd, being inside a stadium for the first time. I was undoubtedly nervous of being in a football crowd, my experience of groups of fans thus far having been more or less limited to the aforementioned unlovely growling multitude of Leeds Utd. However, the happy fandom at that time of the North Stand proved a real energising force and I clearly understood straight away the symbiotic nature of a healthy relationship between players and fans: we adore them, they perform at a level that nurtures and develops that adoration and so the circle is completed: those heady innocent days. In fact, a quick Google reveals that this summertime game drew one of the smaller home attendances of the season with a crowd of 20,879, the only lower crowds were recorded for the games against Coventry and Leicester. Perhaps I wouldn't have been quite so enamoured of a first visit squashed into a crowd of over 32,000 as were there to catch the visits of both Spurs and Liverpool.

When I asked my dad for his memories of the day he said "I can remember how excited you were to see that player you idolised, what was his name? Mariner?" He was right in that I was a huge fan of Mariner, but by the end of the game I was chanting the names of any and all the players: Butcher and Osman for their defensive partnership, Wark, Brazil and Mariner for their goal scoring abilities (all three scored on the day, with Butcher adding the fourth), Mühren and Thijssen for being exotically Dutch and Gates for being little and therefore someone I could relate to (I still have a rather old, slightly scruffy blue and white teddy bear who was always known as Eric because he was rather small).

I also remember looking at my dad and realising the extent of the sacrifice he was making: despite the torrential rain, which lasted for the full ninety minutes, I wanted to stand as close to the pitch as possible. I was reasonably well protected with a classic Seventies orange cagoule. Dad on the other hand had arrived without decent waterproofs and stood stoically in the pouring rain for the duration of the game. I couldn't have known it on the day, but this would be the only time I would make it to Portman Road for many years. I managed to catch a few away games, including a full body armour suited trip to Elland Road to see us lose 3-1 the following March, but for a number of reasons, no more trips to Suffolk for the best part of twenty years. So not only was this my first game, but it was a most treasured memory for years to come.

Having dug out my 1980 diary to see how I had recorded the trip on the day, I flicked through to the end of August and came across something that, as far as I can tell, happened only once in the twelve years or so that I kept a daily diary: I had taped an extra page onto the original small sheet for that day. Having struggled in recent years to maintain a wide-eyed enthusiasm for the club, this extra paper fold is a vivid reminder of how passionate a supporter I was at the time and just how much the club meant to me.

By this age, my diaries are written with a combination of withering sub-Austen asides, a general disdain for the whims of others and a lingering need to record my food intake. The combination leads to an entry on Thursday, 28th August in which the excitement starts to build having eaten chicken liver paté followed by a few hours of watching TV and reading. I then head off to bed having "packed my bag for my assault on Ipswich." Skipping through the relatively straightforward journey to family friends in Colchester who were offering shelter for the nights before and after the game, we move to the excitement-busting, page-adding glory day itself, Saturday. 30th August 1980.

I hand you over to my teenage self:

... after dinner, we caught the train to Ipswich. The ground was about 5 mins away from the station. There was a Portman Road shop and I bought a scarf there before we went in (£1.60 to go in). It poured down nearly the whole time. We were standing where all the noisiest Ipswich fans were and to the right of us, separated by a wire fence, were the Everton fans. The Ipswich players themselves [extra page begins] seemed to prefer our end and Paul Mariner was just about standing on my toes a couple of times, we were right at the front getting soaked. They scored goals in twos, like sneezing, the two at our end being scored by Butcher and Mariner. We won 4-0 (v. Everton) but it wasn't as one sided as it sounds. After the match I went round the back and got the autographs of Franz Thijssen, John Wark and Russell Osman. When I couldn't wait any longer 'cos we had to go and catch the train. [...] Ipswich went 1st in the league. They were on TV too...

Many years later, the goals from the game turned up on an official video produced by the club, somewhat clumsily titled *Right Hammerings*. I've watched the goals back any number of times and if you know where and when to look, sure enough, behind the goal leaping up and down as Terry Butcher and Paul Mariner score, you can just make out a small orange jelly bean shaped blob.

I don't remember seeing Sir Bobby Robson that day - I wish I had. I wish I were one of those lucky fans who have a cherished photograph of the great man standing with his arm draped protectively over a young shoulder. However, attending a Test Match at Lord's Cricket Ground in the early 2000s, I turned around to see a familiar face staring out from the balcony above. More and more of the crowd began to spot him and gradually the chant rose in a manner doubtless not to the approval of those over in the Pavilion, "*One Bobby Robson, there's only one Bobby Robson.*" The man himself looked down at us happily, waved at us benignly (I like to think he spotted my ITFC cap amongst the crowd) and withdrew to the privacy of his box to enjoy the remainder of the game undisturbed.

Don Revie may well have saved my life by building an unsupportable team and thus turning me on to a life of blue in Suffolk, but it was Bobby Robson and his brilliant team of the late Seventies and early Eighties who enriched it in ways that still resonate. I have much to thank him for.

Sarah Rogers

Ipswich Town 4 Everton 0
Division One 1980/81
Attendance: 20,879
Referee: Michael Taylor

IPSWICH TOWN

Manager: Bobby Robson

Team: Paul Cooper, George Burley, Mick Mills,
Frans Thijssen, Russell Osman, Terry Butcher, John Wark,
Arnold Mühren, Paul Mariner, Alan Brazil, Eric Gates. (Subs:
None)

Goals: Brazil (11)
                 Wark (12)
                 Butcher (81)
                 Mariner (83)

EVERTON

Manager: Gordon Lee

Team: Jim McDonagh, John Gidman, Kevin
Ratcliffe, Billy Wright, Mick Lyons, Gary Stanley, Steve
McMahon, Asa Hartford, Bob Latchford, Peter Eastoe, Joe
McBride. (Substitute: Eamon O'Keefe)

FOUR

Chelmsford City 1 Ipswich Town 3
Saturday, 13 January 1973
New Writtle Street

Now, when watching Ipswich play away, it is no surprise to see fans as young as five or six with their parents, but growing up in the Sixties and Seventies, it was rarely seen and, no matter how I nagged my dad, I was never going to be invited on an away trip with him and his mates. He even took mum occasionally but I would be stuck at home. It was not that my dad (or any Town fan) ordinarily went to many run-of the-mill away games in the league at places like Coventry or Newcastle, where the away support for the Town hardly ever reached three figures. Cup games and trips to the capital would see hundreds, and sometimes thousands, of fans attending the matches. By the age of eleven, I was watching most First team home games (not paying, but sneaking in with my dad and sitting on the back of a seat) and I was also a regular at reserve and youth games, but my elusive first away match still seemed years away. Then we had the FA Cup draw for the third round of the 72/73 competition, the draw took place at Monday lunch time and, when I got home from school and asked, I found out we had drawn a non-league team. Trouble is, I did not actually know what a non-league team was! Not only were our opponents to be non-league but we also had a local derby on our hands - not that I really knew what a local derby was - this was still the time we hardly played Norwich and Colchester seemed to play in a parallel universe of Friday night football against teams like Rochdale and Darlington. So we had a non-league opponent, a local derby. But for many reasons, supporters seemed very happy with the draw; special trains were to be ordered, the match would be all ticket and Ipswich sold out their allocation very quickly - most of this information I gathered from the local paper, but it did not seem that would help me get to my first away game. Then dad came home from work and not only did he have match tickets and special train tickets, he also had three sets, so I was going to be going to my first ever away match alongside my dad and mum and, from what the local paper seemed to be hinting at, most of Ipswich would also be taking the short trip down into Essex - many on the special trains but, some would use the A12 and attempt to brave the Army & Navy roundabout (ask your grandparents - think of M25 hold-ups or traffic chaos at Copdock roundabout and double it!) Still at primary school, it seemed I was the only pupil going to the game so I would be the first St Helen's pupil ever to go to an away match! Trouble was, however long we compared our Topps and A&BC football cards in the playground, we could not find one Chelmsford City player. This was many years before the internet and Chelmsford were unlikely to feature in *Shoot* or *Goal* magazine, so it was very hard to find out anything about the Essex club, although they always had a match report in the *Green'Un* so I discovered they played in the Southern League and played the likes of Dover, Margate, Maidstone and Leatherhead and that they drew crowds of just under 3,000 but that was about all I could find out. If the internet had been around, I would have found out that City had a similar history to us, becoming a limited company in the late Thirties they were the big non-league team in the area and were unhappy that both Ipswich and Colchester had beaten them to league status. When we went to play them in 1973, they still harboured hopes of league football and were not averse to spending big money on players with one Jimmy Greaves later to turn up at New Writtle Street. So on 13th January 1973, I joined thousands of other Ipswich fans on the short trip south, not that I knew as an eleven year old, but it seemed trouble was expected. We were met off the train by police and police dogs (not sure I had seen a police dog before). I do remember that the police were quite aggressive and it was not until much later that we all discovered why. Earlier trains had dispatched some of the rowdier Town supporters and they had run amok in the town with two groups of Town fans meeting in Woolworths and causing over £700 of damage to the shop - a figure that would be in the region of £10,000 now. There had also been a number of quite vicious battles between both sets of supporters before the match. As we had arrived on a later train, we were oblivious to all this and we made our way quickly to the ground. The stadium is no longer there, but as you pass through Chelmsford on the train you can still see where the ground was as it sat directly behind the Essex cricket ground, which is far more visible now as it has its own floodlights.

I had already got the programme collector's bug so, on seeing a programme seller, my dad gave me a few pence and I purchased the thin programme. Running back to dad, I discovered I had purchased a pirate programme and my dad threw it away but the cup spirit must have got to him as he gave me some more coins to purchase the official programme. Little did I know that years later you can still pick the official programme up cheaply but the pirate programme could cost you up to £20! We entered the ground and found a place to watch from the side stand; there seemed to be Town fans everywhere! The crowd was over 15,000 - seven times the normal City crowd and most of them seemed to have come from Suffolk. Town fans were in every stand but it seemed there had been more trouble as the City fans had sang "You will never take the Wolseley end" only to be chased out of the stand as 200 Ipswich fans decided that they would not only "take the Wolseley end" but they would then stay in the stand and watch the game with the City fans, either choosing to flee the ground or watch from the open "Scoreboard" end. The teams were announced and the Ipswich team gave a debut to the young John Peddelty, a late replacement for Kevin Beattie who had picked up an injury. Little did we know that was to become the pattern for the rest of Beattie's career.

The game started at a frantic pace, with a fantastic atmosphere; not only my first away game but my first at an almost full house and every stand was singing - something not known at Portman Road. The first goal was a cracker and came from an unlikely source; a Peter Morris free kick was laid back to Colin Harper, playing at left back, who hit it first time with the ball ending up in the top corner of the goal. Harper would eventually end up as player-manager at Chelmsford for a short while. The home team were making a good match of it, with Eddie Dilsworth giving Mills a torrid time. Mills gave a questionable display that day and many Chelmsford supporters would not have believed that nine years later Mills would be captaining his country in the World Cup Finals. Ten minutes before half time, Town got a second when Scouser David Johnson got himself on the score sheet, however City carried on taking the game to Town and we were all happy when the half-time whistle blew.

I'm not sure we had much half-time entertainment before at Portman Road so it was surprise to see some at New Writtle Street! We had an impromptu pitch invasion by the Town fans and the police seemed reluctant to stop it, but the Town fans did not seem to know what to do when they got on to the pitch. Therefore, the large group (mostly teenagers) undertook a number of laps of honour with their leader on the shoulders of the Town fans at the front. My dad gave me a quick glance, which relayed to me via his scowl that I was to stay where I was and in no circumstances was I to join the others on the pitch. However, from afar I was staring intently at the group's leaders with their Doc Marten boots, flared jeans, jean jackets and scarves tied round wrists but most of all it was the main leader who I was drawn to. Knee length, white butcher's coat with Ipswich Town and North Stand painted (badly) on the back of the coat. Where did you get a coat like that? Did you have to get a job as a butcher's assistant on a Saturday? Did the local Co-op sell them? A few months later, when arriving at secondary school, white coats were found in the woodwork, and biology labs, but by then I realised they were not worn at football by the likes of eleven year olds!

Half-time over, the Town fans made their way back to the Wolseley end and the game started again, and after seventy-five minutes, Town added a third, scored by Bryan Hamilton. Mick Mills may have had a torrid time at the back but it was his control of the ball in midfield and his pass that made the third goal. Nowadays, going two up would have been the signal to start substituting a number of players, but in the days of just one sub it was only the Essex side that put a substitute on and in the eighty-ninth minute, City got what was a deserved consolation goal. When the final whistle went, there was no pitch invasion as everyone left the ground quickly with most Town fans heading towards the train station. I thought it was good game, but many Town fans were disappointed that we did not score more and Robson was also not impressed as he kept the team in the dressing room after the game to tear a few strips off them. Some had expected a possible cup shock so much so that ITV had filmed the game, which was the main match on Anglia's *Match of the Week* and even made the second game on LWT's *Big Match*. You can even find the *Big Match* episode for this week on the internet, so you can listen to what Jimmy Hill and Brian Moore thought of the match. The first game on the programme was the Brighton-Chelsea cup game where Peter Osgood was outstanding.

Little did we know when we watched the highlights on Sunday afternoon that on Monday lunchtime we would be drawn out of the hat to play Chelsea away in the fourth round. I must have behaved on the day as my dad and his mates allowed me to join them on the special train to Liverpool Street for the fouth round Cup game in West London. Another packed train as thousands of Town supporters made their way to Chelsea but not surprisingly this time there was no pitch invasion by the Ipswich support or any sign of the rabble-rouser and his white coat, maybe he could not get off his shift at the local butchers that week. The trouble at the match was covered intensely over the next few months in the local papers, with a number of high profile court cases. It seemed to come as a shock to most fans as Ipswich supporters had a good name. As we were the larger team, most of the blame seemed to fall on Ipswich and our supporters. When the cases came to court, it was not just Ipswich supporters who were found guilty, but also supporters from Chelmsford and Colchester. This was for many Town fans the first real trouble they had seen at a football match, but something that we were going to get used to seeing, with Ipswich fans mainly the innocent party with the London clubs, Manchester United (and their Cockney Reds), Leeds and Liverpool bringing most of the trouble to Town. Not to say Ipswich were totally innocent as trouble at Norwich and friendlies in Colchester and Cambridge was more akin to the scenes at Chelmsford, with Ipswich fans often being the perpetrators. My dad would not take me at the end of the season to the Texaco Cup final, second leg at Norwich as he seemed to know there would be trouble. I never spoke to him for weeks as I moaned that I had missed probably the only time we would ever win a cup. Fortunately, I was very wrong on that front. Hooliganism would continue to blight the game throughout the Seventies and early Eighties with Ipswich fans on the receiving end of one of the worst cases at another FA Cup match, this time at Millwall in 1978. As this was my first ever away game, it is still one of my most memorable ever Town games. I do not want to glorify the trouble, but as a very impressionable eleven year old the trouble that day was part of why the game became so memorable. Looking back on the pictures of the day it does show you how far we have come as football supporters. The pictures also give us a snapshot of what policing (and football) was like in the early Seventies; no replica shirts, but flared jeans, boots, long hair and scarves tied round wrists. In those days police patrolled in a variety of uniforms and the cars were not fast pursuit vehicles like today, but small minis, reminding us now of shows like *Cars*. Pitch wise, it bought back memories of the first good Robson teams with young players coming through to play alongside seasoned pros like Peter Morris. This was a team that would go on to win the Texaco Cup and be the nucleus of our first FA Cup semi-final side. Kevin Beattie missed the game, a sign that already we had a player who would suffer more than others would from injury. His replacement that day, John Peddelty would move to Plymouth as part of the deal that saw Paul Mariner arrive in Suffolk. John also had to retire from the game early due to a head injury but he would return to the town to become a local police officer.

The other memory the game brings back to me is of watching football with my parents, both gone now but they passed on the love of this football club to me. I am so glad that we could share events like this together- even if on this day it may have been more about what happened off the pitch than the cup win against our non-league neighbours.

Alasdair Ross

Chelmsford City 1 Ipswich Town 3
FA Cup, Third Round, 1972/73
Attendance: 15,557
Referee: Iorwerth P. Jones

CHELMSFORD CITY

Manager: Dave Bumpstead

Team: Laurie Taylor, Tommy Coakley, Vic Gomersall, Paul Delea, Mick Loughton, Len Tomkins, Bernie Lewis, Terry Price, Roy Woolcott, Frank Peterson, Eddie Dilsworth (Sub: Barry Thornley)

Goals: Woolcott (89)

IPSWICH TOWN

Manager: Bobby Robson

Team: David Best, Mick Mills, Colin Harper, Peter Morris, Allan Hunter, John Peddelty, Bryan Hamilton, Colin Viljoen, Dave Johnson, Trevor Whymark, Mick Lambert (Substitute: none)

Goals: Harper (9)
          Johnson (35)
          Hamilton (75)

FIVE

Foggia 0 Ipswich Town 1
Wednesday, 8 November 1995
Stadio Pino Zaccheria

I was embarrassingly over-excited when I heard that Ipswich Town would be taking part in the Anglo-Italian Cup. I was too young to have watched Ipswich play in the UEFA Cup in the early eighties, and was envious of my Dad's tales of watching our UEFA Cup victory in the Netherlands. I started watching Ipswich regularly in the Bobby Ferguson and John Duncan era, so genuinely thought that the Anglo-Italian Cup would be my only hope of ever watching Ipswich play abroad.

This fixture also provided me with my first opportunity to travel abroad without my parents. I was twenty years old and working as a care assistant in Bury St Edmunds. Still paying back my grant after dropping out of university, and due to start my nurse training a couple of months later, it was trip I could ill-afford, but I was determined to go. It was as big a deal for me as the UEFA Cup had been for my Dad.

I knew nothing about how to organise a trip abroad, so got together with a few other regulars from the Bury away supporters' bus and our rag-bag group was formed. Brabs and Iain from school, Jacko the Bury Branch legend and professional smoker who had recently introduced me to the delights of Whiskey Mac, and Betty and Eddie from the Haverhill branch.

We looked at a map to find out where Foggia is, saw that we could get a package deal to Sorrento and thought "that'll do us." It was in the south, and although it was on the opposite coast it looked easy. I mean, how wide could Italy be?

We made the match by sheer fluke. None of us had any idea how we would get to Foggia, or how long the journey would take. We decided to set out from Sorrento early on match day. Just as well as it turned out Italy is actually quite wide, and there are mountains to get across so getting from Napoli to Bari was in fact going to take at least six hours.

The train journey was a great experience. We were in an old-style carriage, six seats facing each other and a sliding door into a corridor, the kind I'd only seen in films. It was starting to feel like a proper adventure.

I went to the toilet and came back to find Jacko had disappeared into the next compartment. I could hear various voices: "John Wark," the clinking of glass bottles, "Arnold Mühren," more clinking. Jacko had, in the few minutes I'd been gone, befriended the Polish soldiers in the next carriage, who had a large hold-all of beer. The language barrier no object, they conversed and drank for several hours. The conversation consisting of listing any footballer they had all heard of, followed by the clinking of bottles. I was in awe of how many different languages Jacko could say "cheers" in.

We somehow arrived in Bari just in time for a connection to Foggia, and made kick-off with a little bit of time to spare. I remember more about the pre-match build up than I do the actual match, which probably says all you need to know about the quality of the game. Word had got round that at the previous Italian fixture in Brescia, club chairman David Sheepshanks had bought a pint for all of the Ipswich fans who had made the journey. There were about fifty-two of us, expectant. Sheepshanks arrived, ruddy faced as usual. No sign of the wallet coming out. A chant went up of "Sheepshanks, where's our beer, Sheepshanks, Sheepshanks, where's our beer." It was all very good natured, but the wallet stayed firmly in his pocket.

A quick look around the assembled Ipswich fans and I noticed the group I'd named the "Chelmsford Punks." I'd admired them from a distance since I graduated from the lower Pioneer Stand to the North Stand five years earlier. For me they were the cool grown-ups of the North Stand. The best hair, and best clothes. The woman who I secretly aspired to be (she always had brilliant shoes) slept, I think, through the entire game, laid across several seats, with a leather jacket placed across her by the rest of her group. And I mean slept solidly. It was the most impressive sleeping I'd ever witnessed. The ten minutes that preceded the start of the sleep was also the drunkest that I'd ever seen anyone.

The team came out to warm up, and seemed to be a bit bemused and awkward in the fairly large but very empty stadium. We got a nice reaction from Tony Vaughan who had a bit of friendly, shouted exchange with us. We'd beaten Reading 4-1 in our previous match, a game memorable for most Ipswich fans because of Geraint "George" Williams' goal, where he'd picked up the ball from the half-way line, gone on a mazy run and buried it. The most un-Williams thing he'd ever done in his career. Chants of "Williams from the half-way line" grew. He looked chuffed. After we'd kept it going for a few minutes, he decided to do a re-enactment for us. He placed the ball on the half-way line, dodged his way past imaginary defenders and scored past the imaginary keeper, then re-enacted his celebration. Some of his team mates piled in with the celebration, others just stood about laughing. It's still one of the favourite things I've ever seen in my thirty-four years of watching Ipswich Town.

I don't remember too much about the actual match! We won 1-0 and Paul Mason scored. I had to look this up though, as I thought it might have been Tony Vaughan. The crowd was small (2,000) but noisy, and I was impressed that the Foggia fans could even be bothered to bring a couple of flares to such an underwhelming fixture.

After the match me and Brabs got separated from our group. We wandered about for a while until we had to agree we were actually lost. We couldn't find anyone, or a bus or train station so we wandered back near to the ground. We saw the team bus outside a hotel, so went into the hotel bar. The whole was squad in there. Mauricio Taricco was tucked away in a corner, deep in conversation with someone, who I presumed was his dad, with a bottle of red wine, full strength Marlboro on the go. He was already my hero. That sealed the deal for the long-term. We chatted to a couple of players who were all friendly and engaging, and Tony Vaughan and David Gregory bought us a pint.

I explained to the kit-man Trevor Kirton that we were lost and separated from our group and needed to get to railway station to get the night train back, and asked if they were going anywhere near the station and if we could have a lift. He went to speak to a couple of people and it was all sorted. Brabs was totally embarrassed. We were ushered on to the bus after everyone else had got on so we had to make our way down the bus to find a spare seat, like one of those awkward school trip experiences. I sat behind Craig Forrest and Micky Stockwell. Sheepshanks came down and checked we were OK. The team dropped us off at the station, and found our friends there waiting on the platform ready for the night train back to Napoli, drifting in and out of sleep.

We arrived back in the UK on Friday 10th, shattered, but we'd all decided to go to Millwall away the following day. In truth we were feeling pretty smug about having made the trip, and partly went to brag: "*If you all went to Foggia, clap your hands.*"

Much to my surprise, I did get another opportunity to watch Ipswich play in Europe, when we unfathomably qualified for the UEFA Cup five years later. I went to watch the away matches in Moscow and Milan, but didn't enjoy either experience as much as my Foggia adventure.

Emma Corlett

Foggia 0 Ipswich Town 1
Anglo-Italian Cup, League Stage 1995/96
Attendance: c. 2,000
Referee: Billy Burns

FOGGIA

Manager: Delio Rossi

Team: Alex Brunner, Donatello Gasparini, Joseph Oshadogan, Giuseppe Di Bari, Aniello Parisi, Massimiliano Giacobbo, Noccolo Sciacca, Aldo Di Corcia, Giuseppe Anastasi, Luca Amoruso, Massimo Marazzina (Subs: Gualtiero Grandini, Igor Kolyvanov, Pasquale De Vincenzo)

IPSWICH TOWN

Manager: George Burley

Team: Craig Forrest, Mick Stockwell, John Wark, Tony Mowbray, Mauricio Taricco, Adam Tanner, Geraint Williams, Neil Gregory, Simon Milton, Lee Chapman, Paul Mason (Subs: Claus Thomsen, Stuart Slater)

Goals: Mason (26)

SIX

Millwall 1 Ipswich Town 6
Saturday, 11 March 1978
The Den

I cannot claim to have predicted much during the turbulence that turned out to be the 1970s. Life took me by surprise: The Beatles splitting up, England being thwarted by a Polish goalkeeper, the turn to Punk. Falling in love with the same girl twice yet still getting it wrong, both times. I was pretty young and pretty vacant.

But I spotted that bottle. From a point far left, it traced a graceful arc. The backdrop was frozen, its actors were frozen, I was frozen ... but that bottle kept tumbling. Bottle-neck, bottle-base, bottle-neck, bottle-base, clockwise: tumbling.

It should have whistled to warn us: like bombs dropping thirty-four years before onto U-boat pens under cliffs at Brest, onto the brazen metal spaghetti of Marseille's marshalling yards, on the helpless German civilians of the Ruhr's "happy valley." On people. On other people. Bombs dropped by a nineteen-year-old man who since then had not just become a father: he had become my father.

But this little beauty, this little bomb, was spinning to us. Even as a policeman braced the grey metal door from behind, a zigzag of serge muscle in blue-clad right angles; and another policeman shouted into his radio whilst leaning, buttress-style, into the same door as his mate. Even the policemen seemed still figures in a raging storm. But the bottle span on.

It span towards me, who was still; towards those around me, who were still; towards my father on my left, who had taken that position the moment the trouble had started. He was neither still, nor agitated. He just leaned a fraction further right; the better to shield me, the more to risk himself.

And as he leant, it dropped. The moment splintered. The bottle picked its target, to be the seat in front. It was occupied by a woman much older than me, perhaps older even than my father. Her hair was dark, like my mother's, permed into waves but with wisps of grey. Chatting earlier it turned out she had travelled from Suffolk, on one of the scores of coaches commissioned by supporters. She had made such journeys on many occasions. Today's trip would be different, she hoped, for neither the woman nor the team she followed, had much joy in that season's travels. The league campaign of 1977-78 may have been in the top flight, but it was disappointing. Town eventually squeaked clear of relegation by two places and three points, with just a single away win at Newcastle. Norwich finished in thirteenth place, just below Manchester United. Brian Clough's Nottingham Forest won the league title seven points clear of Liverpool, who were trailed by Everton, Manchester City and Arsenal.

Yet despite and in retrospect being a team in transition, this Ipswich side could hit some remarkable high spots. Beating Norwich four-nil was a local one; and thrashing Barcelona three-nil at Portman Road proved a European sensation. That November evening in 1977 was unforgettable, despite the subsequent disappointment of losing the away leg to Spanish penalties.

But what of this March Saturday, four months on? Of the afternoon in which that bottle hovers, fateful, above a woman's head? Of a father leant unflinching, to protect his son?

The footballing truth was that despite two eventually glorious finals in the Robson era, at this point Town were not an outstanding cup team. That was why this moment mattered. Thanks to beating Cardiff, Hartlepool and the gallant Bristol Rovers, by 3pm on that March afternoon in 1978 Ipswich were just two games away from Wembley; and through the luck of the draw facing a struggling side from the division below them, in an FA Cup quarter final. Only these were not just any opponents, and this was not just a random ground. The team to beat was Millwall and this was *The Den*, down Cold Blow Lane.

The first casualties, including several fatalities, happened before the match had even kicked off. Bizarre though it may seem to our twenty-first century-selves, and in a misguided attempt to provide twentieth-century "family entertainment" for the bumper crowd, Millwall's management team had laid on half an hour of simulated, but nevertheless realistic and extreme physical gang violence. At about 2.15pm a gaggle of "Cowboys" in Stetson hats, waistcoats and fringed suede jackets, mysteriously appeared at one end of the pitch, shortly to be joined from the other end by a party of attacking "Indians." Given it was 1978 these were called "Red Indians" (not "Native Americans") and could easily be distinguished by their feather headdresses, lurid war paint, whooping and drumming. Oh, and getting shot by the Cowboys, whose pistols and rifles emitted convincing cracks of gunfire and real smoke. My 1978-self did not register exactly what happened to the Native American dead: but I distinctly recall a fallen Cowboy being heaved into an authentic-looking wooden coffin. Yes, an actual coffin. On the pitch at Millwall. Before the game had even kicked off; and as family entertainment.

A raw recruit from Scotland (George Burley) had been watching this pre-match fun. From it he took his cue. Once the dead Americans had been hauled off the pitch, to be replaced at 3pm by twenty-two professional, living and more suitably dressed combatants, it was he who pulled the first trigger. Ten minutes into the game and from deep inside the Millwall half, Burley galloped like a cavalryman into green empty space. Then into more space, then into a few more yards of apparently unoccupied South London Reservation before: crack! Not so much a handgun as a long range, right-footed rifling of a goal. It barrelled into the goalkeeper's top corner from at least twenty-five yards out. If he had seen it coming he was a better player than his defenders; clearly, none of them had.

Given such a rare and astonishing goal from Burley, celebrations from the Ipswich fans were understandable. In the seated section (where my father had, on safety grounds, deliberately purchased our tickets) these consisted of cheering, clapping and waving scarves. In the rest of the ground they were wilder; dangerously wilder. Supporters jumped up and down. Their flags were unfurled. They even sang songs. It was almost as though they were unaware of local customs, of unwritten rules; hadn't they watched *PANORAMA*?

For readers lucky enough to have escaped the 1970s, let me explain. *Panorama* was BBC TV's flagship current affairs programme, an in-depth and more or less peak time televisual exploration of pressing social, economic or political "issues." In late 1977 it had devoted thirty-five minutes of national broadcasting to an undercover film (easily available online via YouTube) exploring the relatively recent phenomenon, of widespread and organised football hooliganism. Over the previous decade, violence from some crowd members had become a growing problem not just for football as a sport, but for society as a whole. *Panorama* had chosen to examine the issue, and explore possible links with the recent rise of the proto-Fascist National Front. They did this not by following around one of England's larger clubs, but through filming at Millwall games, home and away.

Naively, and in an apparent belief that they had recently been getting on top of what had been a recurrent local problem, Millwall's management team offered the BBC unrestricted access. They supported the Corporation's efforts to film both official and several unofficial groups, into which Millwall's fans organised themselves. Millwall's board hoped through *Panorama* to portray themselves as a forward-looking, community-focused club that was both eager to change and willing to "take on" the hooligans.

Instead, the BBC's documentary brought the attention of people who watched serious TV, to the existence of a world which seemed alien and barbaric. Backed up by interviews and apparently authentic crowd shots, filmed in various locations, it taught viewers about: **The Half Way Line** (youngsters), about **The Treatment** (in their surgical masks) and **F Troop**. In best BBC English, F Troop were described as "*Self-confessed loonies like Harry the Dog, who go looking for fights and are seldom disappointed ... in a constant search for excitement and sensation that will make these kids' lives seem less humdrum.*"

The interviewer then, apparently reasonably, asked "*Why don't opposing fans come to Millwall's ground?*" The Treatment's twenty-one-year-old Billy helpfully explained from behind thick glasses, perched on a tank top and framed by shoulder length frizzy hair "*Because they'd get battered.*" A young visiting Blackburn fan, who had recently experienced one of Billy's batterings, an hour and a half before kick-off and shortly after arriving in South London, vouched ruefully for the claim.

"*Because of Millwall's reputation other fans tend to stay at home,*" the voiceover concluded. And as their young, modern-looking, manager Gordon Jago confirmed, that was one of the main reasons why he and Herbert Burnidge, a senior club director, had agreed to collaborate with the BBC's film makers.

They were desperate to showcase how club-community links were being nurtured, that the Club was talking with and attempting to control its fans: that as an organisation Millwall did not want and would not tolerate hooliganism at its matches. On camera and as part of the programme, Jago told an interviewer that if Millwall could find a way to build a new all-seater stadium, from which offending fans could be excluded and in which bad behaviour could more easily be controlled, they would without hesitation. Such a stadium could be *"safe for away fans"*. Jago was even pictured attempting to convince groups of young Millwall supporters, that if more away followers could be persuaded to visit The Den he could use the increased revenue to buy a new centre forward.

In 1977 all-seater stadia were, in England, a long way into the future. But Ipswich Town's visit to the ramshackle terraces and small grandstands of The Den happened just a few months after *Panorama* was broadcast. Unwittingly their FA Cup quarter final visit would enable notoriety to be cemented, for the small but significant minority of Millwall fans who had been publicised four months earlier on national prime time TV.

In a storm of controversy and flooded also by football failure, Gordon Jago resigned just after *Panorama* documentary was aired. His part in the decision to offer the BBC open access was seen as naïve and damaging. Local confidence in the wider management team was also low. Arguably "Harry the Dog," pathetic a character as he appeared in the documentary, carried as much authority at the moment of Ipswich's visit, as anybody else at Millwall. And what better way to seize fame, to secure that storyline, to broadcast that myth, than for him and other gang members to star once more via national TV and newspapers, as "defenders of The Den?" South London cowboys, taking on East Anglian Indians?

I am not certain, if I am honest, precisely where the trouble started. I had been too busy watching the weird Wild West show, and then George Burley's wonder goal. But just after that, ominous gaps started to appear in various crowded terraces. Millwall's fans were charging the police, and attacking any Ipswich fans they could reach. That was not too difficult given that, in our Suffolk naïvety, thousands of us had travelled to watch from various stands; but if they could not break through police lines, or clamber over fences for face-to-face fighting, the Millwall gang members started throwing whatever objects they could find, at any Ipswich fans they could see. That was when the referee decided, a mere eighteen minutes into the match and on the grounds of "public safety" to take the players off the pitch.

Only with no Cowboys, no Indians and now not even any football to watch, public safety was far from secured. The gang members who had started the trouble were now free to concentrate upon sustaining it, and pursue their prime interests: self-promotion and self-glorification through inflicting random violence, on innocent people. That's why those two policemen found themselves heroically barricading a metal door, against desperate attempts by countless others to breach it. Thwarted by such bravery, that is also why missiles started to rain down from the other side of the divide: onto the seats in the grandstand occupied by Ipswich fans.

Bottle-neck, bottle-base. Bottle-neck, bottle-base. Bottle bomb: a cartwheeling ellipse from the left, hovering for a moment above the unprotected head of a middle-aged woman. Then like famous bombs before it, spun onto water in 1943 from the planes of 617 Squadron; the same planes in which my father flew hundreds of hours strapped inside a tiny rear turret, turrets from which they hosed out the shredded flesh of fallen heroes...

It bounced.

The bottle, bounced. Neither neck nor base landed, on unprotected skull, to fracture bone, or cleave cranium, or bite into brain. The smooth side of the bottle skimmed off her scalp. It bruised but it neither smashed, nor cut. None of us saw where it went. For by that time we were all cowering, low into the seats, into the floor, our coats or jumpers or newspapers pathetically held aloft above the precious cranial bowls within which we were trying to work out: why? Why the hell are they doing this?

Within a minute or two police reinforcements had arrived. Truncheons were drawn. A charge cleared the troublemakers back, through a hapless throng of scared and often innocent Millwall fans, some of whom, through no fault of their own, were also injured. Then a quarter of an hour after that, following a break of nineteen minutes in the game, more police and the match officials led the players back onto the pitch. Play resumed. The referee was determined, and made it known over the public address system, that he would not allow crowd violence to force an abandonment.

So why, you might ask, was this a great game?

Partly because by sheer good fortune the woman in front of me, miraculously, was not even injured by a missile that could have killed her. Or killed my father, or me. That was no consolation to the scores of other Ipswich fans who were terrified, assaulted and in some cases badly injured before, during and after the game: but it means I can look back without a memory of physical pain.

On a personal level that game was also special because for the first time in my life, I witnessed my father's physical bravery. He was a slim, quietly spoken and gentle man, who as a child I had never seen playing sport or confronting others. It was not until the shared jeopardy of that afternoon, when he appeared totally untroubled by the surrounding chaos, that I realised what (real) war had taught him: to be utterly unafraid of injury or death. Or perhaps more accurately, to appear that way.

Yet what offered the widest consolation, to most visitors from Suffolk, was the way in which that Ipswich team played. Millwall's footballers may have been "inferior opposition," but the bottles, bricks and other missiles flung by their gang members nearly hit several Ipswich players. It was not just the fans who were in danger. Nor can it have been much fun as a footballer to sit in that dressing room, during nineteen postponed minutes, listening to the distant sounds of chaos whilst knowing that soon you would be back at its sharp end: ready to face at least eighty minutes of further hostile, and potentially violent attention. And to do all that whilst concentrating, performing and winning. Yet that was precisely what the Ipswich team managed to achieve. Paul Mariner added second and third goals in the fifty-second and seventy-second minutes. That brace was followed by a Millwall consolation, then three Ipswich goals during the final three minutes: one of which completed a Mariner hat trick.

Those goals sealed, at 1-6, the most emphatic FA Cup quarter final result for over fifty years. Ipswich Town's courage and coolness had ensured that, at least during the game, their football did the fighting.

Yet the intensity and disquiet of that awful afternoon was, within hours, on national display. Interviewed for BBC's *Match of the Day* shortly after the game had finished, a visibly shaken Bobby Robson had vented his disgust and frustration at this assault, on a sport to which he had devoted his life. *"They should have flamethrowers turned on them,"* Robson said bitterly when trying to describe his feelings, about the troublemakers. He did not mean it literally and had withdrawn the comment by the morning of the next day. But such anger was typical of the frustration felt by many at the time, from all sides. Herbert Burnidge, the Chairman of Millwall and a key advocate for the reforming spirit espoused (at least on TV) by Gordon Jago, resigned soon after.

Many innocent Millwall fans, as well as Ipswich, were terrorised or hurt in the chaos; and millions saw the images in newspapers or on TV. Was society descending into anarchy? Within fifteen months, Margaret Thatcher had swept into power via an electoral landslide. For years after she rode a rising tide of authoritarian populism and free market promises, successfully in many voters's minds associating social disorder and industrial unrest, with liberal attitudes and a state that gave its citizens welfare. Yet despite the rhetoric of condemnation from her three governments, more than a decade would pass before any radical changes were made in football: and those only happened years after (and because of) the tragedy at Hillsborough in 1989.

The subsequent Taylor Report from 1990 did eventually change everything, in football grounds and for football fans. Yet by then the periodic and well-publicised instances of 1970s and 1980s football-related public disorder, had played their own small part in persuading three parliament's worth of voters that Britain needed "strong Tory government," that a "shrinking state" and "more prisons and police" and "weaker unions" and an actual war with Argentina, were constructive ways to improve peoples' lives. It is ironic that Margaret Thatcher's 1987 remark *"You know, there's no such thing as society. There are individual men and women, and there are families,"* now seems almost as irrational as the antics of Harry the Dog, from a decade before: disorderly behaviour from which Thatcher's own authoritarianism had derived so many of its justifications.

Any game in any successful cup run is, of course, arguably as important as all the others. But of the three trips Ipswich Town made to London in March, April and then May 1978, on their way to winning the FA Cup, that March visit to The Den at Millwall was pivotal. It hinted to me, to many other Ipswich fans and perhaps even to our players, that something special could happen: whatever the opposing team might throw at us

Grant Bage

Millwall 1 Ipswich Town 6
FA Cup Quarter Final 1977/78
Attendance: 23,082
Referee: John Gow

MILLWALL

Manager: George Petchey

Team: Nicky Johns, Dave Donaldson, Jon Moore, Phil Walker, Barry Kitchener, Tony Hazell, Ian Pearson, Bian Chambers, Bryan Hamilton, Trevor Lee, Roger Cross. (Sub: David Mehmet)

Goals: Mehmet (84)

IPSWICH TOWN

Manager: Bobby Robson

Team: Paul Cooper, George Burley, Mick Mills, Brian Talbot, Allan Hunter, Russell Osman, John Wark, Paul Mariner, Robin Turner, Clive Woods.(Sub: Mick Lambert).

Goals: George Burley (10)
               Paul Mariner (52, 72, 89)
               John Wark (87)
               Brian Talbot (88)

SEVEN

Ipswich Town 5 Bolton Wanderers 3
Wednesday, 17 May 2000
Portman Road

Timing. You're either got it or you haven't. Some people - I'm one of them - seem fated to live their lives arriving at a bonfire party just as the fireworks are finishing, or turning on the TV just after someone breaks the world 100m record, or getting to a buffet table the very nanosecond after someone has snaffled the last chicken drumstick.

I've known from an early age that I'm one of these people, because I started watching Ipswich in the 1982/83 season, which is pretty much the exact equivalent of getting to an Elbow gig just as the final chords of *One Day Like This* are crashing round the arena. Bobby Robson had just gone, and the team that he built was steadily following him out of the door. My dad and other family members had been telling me how amazing it was to watch Mühren, Thijssen, Mariner and the others in full flow, but by the time I was old enough to go to the party, the empty beer cans and crisps were being swept away, and time had very definitely been called at the title-chasing bar.

For the rest of my childhood, things got steadily worse at Portman Road: playing standards dropped, crowds dwindled, and each year's Junior Blues membership package seemed a bit more disappointing than the last. The free-scoring Ipswich who regularly competed for top honours, which I had heard and read so much about, seemed further and further away. All of this coincided with a religious upbringing, so I was well used to being asked to believe in things that I couldn't see or discern, but by the time we got to the John Duncan era, four-figure crowds for home games, Chris O'Donnell and Graham Harbey at full-back, and a team that had the dwindling number of reporters present at Portman Road scrambling to find new synonyms for "mediocre," it was becoming impossible to conceive of a time when Town fans would once again be enthralled, excited and delighted by their team.

In the early 1990s, we unexpectedly got promoted, only to stink the top division out with utterly cynical tactics. By this time, I was editing a Town fanzine, and we would regularly get letters from opposition fans who'd say that we were the worst team they'd ever seen at the top level. Not necessarily the least competent, just the most joyless. "How can you watch that every week?" they would ask. They weren't the only ones: Ipswich were in the Premier League but getting crowds of 15,000. In 1995, eleven people in blue shirts lost 9-0 at Old Trafford, and some of them couldn't have seemed less bothered about it. This was a club that had indisputably lost its mojo.

By the late 1990s, something had started to happen. George Burley had presided over that nonathrashing by Manchester United, and the inevitable relegation which followed, and decided to act. Out of the playing squad went the complacent, the disinterested, and the allegedly-too-frequently-lubricated. In came a sprinkling of astute signings and a steady flow of talent from the youth system. More importantly, Burley had the team playing in a bold, expansive style. Goals flowed, and the team seemed to be taking genuine pleasure in their work. It had taken my entire childhood and adolescence to get there, but finally I was watching a team that Ipswich fans could truly be proud of, and could get behind with passion.

They were flawed, were Burley's Ipswich, and had a particular propensity for self-destruction around the spring time of each season, but we loved them, and greeted each season's nearly-but-not-quite tilt at promotion with appreciation. We wanted to go up, of course we did, but if waiting was the price we were going to have to pay for promotion with style, then we were going to enjoy that wait. Each year's noble but doomed shot at the play-offs - the decade ended with three consecutive semi-final failures - seemed to strengthen the bond between the team and its fans, and renew our collective determination for the next season's attempt.

Because this is the point about my favourite game. It's not just that it was utterly, totally, thrilling (although it was). It's not just that it was a mad-arsed, utterly unpredictable two hours with more interwoven narrative threads than a Coen Brothers movie (although it was). It's not just that it was the triumph of good over Sam Allardyce (although it was). It's that it was, in every sense, an epic climax - not just of the play-offs, not just of that season, but of everything that had gone before, all that we had been through together in the preceding years. It was the night that everything came together, and our collective faith - Burley's faith in playing the way that Bobby Robson had taught him, and our faith in Burley - was gloriously repaid.

May 2000 was the second consecutive year that we'd faced Bolton in the play-off semi-final. In the first leg at Bolton, Town had come back from two goals down to earn a 2-2 draw, leaving us in the unfamiliar and frankly uncomfortable position of going into the home leg as favourites. Not even Manu Thetis's prolonged attempt to hit the Ipswich self-destruct button by dribbling the ball across his own box, for no apparent reason other than he felt like making things more interesting, could keep us from parity. We went into that second leg knowing that we were unlikely to get a better chance to reach the Wembley final that we'd so doggedly swerved for the previous three years.

It would be slightly misleading to portray the contest as stylish sophisticates against knuckle-scraping oafs, but only slightly. Bolton's game-plan - to bully Town out of the high-pressure games, just as Sheffield United and Charlton had done before them - had worked in 1999, and their manager Sam Allardyce saw no reason to change that approach. Only six minutes had gone when Portman Road's rapidly-expanding bubble of noise and expectation was uncompromisingly popped by Robbie Elliott's clattering challenge on Richard Wright, leaving Dean Holdsworth to prod the ball home and put Bolton ahead. Disappointment was tinged with a certain amount of comforting familiarity - if we were going to do it, we were going to do it the hard way.

Referee Barry Knight had studied Elliott's challenge on Wright and deemed it legal - which, to be fair, it probably was. But Knight's early display of latitude clearly encouraged Bolton to step up their game - that game being an unstructured cross between Aussie Rules football and a playground rampage by eleven school bullies on a sugar rush. A few minutes later, Jim Magilton exchanged passes with David Johnson on the edge of the box and was hacked down by Holdsworth. There wasn't even any particular reason for Bolton's centre-forward to be defending at that point. It was just one of those evenings where tactics and reason gave way to almost-constant chaos.

The foul which gave away that first penalty of the evening was a long way from being the dirtiest challenge by a Bolton player that night, but it was symptomatic of the evening. Town were sticking to their principles, keeping the ball, passing-and-moving: Bolton had been so comprehensively drilled to kick us out of our stride that Holdsworth's clumsy roundhouse back-heel into Magilton's shins seemed instinctive. It was a blatant foul, but Bolton's outrage at the penalty award betrayed the instructions that they'd clearly been given. "How can you punish us, ref?" they seemed to be saying, "this is how we're supposed to play." Their reaction was exacerbated, admittedly, by Magilton's enthusiastic baiting of the apoplectic Wanderers defender Mike Whitlow - to the extent that most of the players ended up in one of those mass pushing-and-shouting-and-pointing gatherings which commentators tell us is "the sort of thing that we don't want to see" even though it's exactly the sort of thing that most fans want to see.

Let's pause for a moment to contemplate the underappreciated genius of Jim Magilton. He'd found himself out of favour at Sheffield Wednesday the previous season, after Ron Atkinson had taken over at Hillsborough. "What on earth did you sign him for? He's got the turning circle of an ocean liner," Atkinson is said to have asked of his Wednesday predecessor, David Pleat. "Yes, but he can pass," came Pleat's instant reply. Pleat was right. Magilton was arguably the missing piece in Burley's Ipswich jigsaw: alongside the relentless efficiency of Matt Holland in midfield, Magilton was all technique. The coherence of the team around him created the space for Magilton to thrive: likewise, Magilton's constant hunger for the ball, and his ability to think two or three passes ahead when laying it off, provided a stage for his team-mates to express themselves on.

While Magilton's playing style was a testament to the discipline that he'd been taught in his formative years at Anfield, his personal approach to the game was somewhere between an over-excitable toddler and Begbie from *Trainspotting*: an all-encompassing enthusiasm which somehow left him permanently on the verge of a fight. Such qualities demanded the near-constant attention of his team-mates - whether they were finding the space in which to receive one of his pin-point passes, or pulling him away from yet another face-to-face screaming match with an opponent.

Nights like the 2000 play-off semi-final were made for Magilton. Thriving on the knife-edge atmosphere that others might have shrunk from, and bringing his team-mates with him via the sheer force of his personality, he had the sort of evening which, had it been scripted as the final scene of a low-budget TV movie called The Jim Magilton Story, *would have been rejected as too far-fetched. Having won the penalty, and - just as importantly - properly got Bolton's backs up in the process, he proceeded to straighten his collar, pick up the ball and smash it expertly into Jussi Jääskeläinen's net. 3-3 on aggregate, and we'd barely got started. It wasn't, however, going to be the sort of evening in which anyone could sit back and admire the sun setting behind the West Stand. Having dared to think that the home side might perhaps take control of the contest, Town were behind again. Referee Knight awarded Bolton a free-kick on the edge of the box: a well-drilled set-piece routine deceived Wright, and Holdsworth curled the ball into the corner of the net.*

Then, before half-time, just in case anyone was starting to get bored, another penalty. This time it was Marcus Stewart who had the momentary use of his legs decisively taken away from him by Paul Ritchie. Bolton's protests were so fervent that the club stewards intervened to protect the referee. Before the kick was taken, there was time for yet another spat between Magilton and a Wanderers' player, this time Paul Warhurst. Magilton sent the kick the same way as his earlier one, but Jääskeläinen won the psychological battle, guessing correctly and turning the ball around the post.

So Ipswich were behind again, and the assembled reporters had a chance to prepare their so-near-yet-so-far pieces while enjoying the half-time refreshments.

For supporters of my generation, who grew up watching Ipswich on

Saturdays and Bobby Robson's England in between times, the epic, heroic failure had become the highest level of achievement, a kind of prized sporting currency all of its own. The 1990 World Cup was a prime example: our teams weren't the sort of teams who actually won things, but they were the sort of teams who made a lung-busting, heart-rending go of just missing out. At half-time that night at Portman Road in May 2000, the anticipation of sloping away with no reward except a perceived moral victory was beginning to wrap itself around us like a comfort blanket. At least we wouldn't get all the way to Wembley and lose. We could go home knowing that we'd tried our best to win the right way, but the nasty bullies from Bolton were going to win out in the end, and that's just the way that things were.

That's what we thought, anyway. Someone in the Ipswich dressing room hadn't read the script. Town nearly equalised straight from the second-half kick-off, James Scowcroft going close with a header. A few minutes, later, we were back level with the most un-Jim Magilton goal of Jim Magilton's entire career. Picking up the ball on the edge of the box, Magilton found himself with no time or space to attempt one of his trademark through-balls, so was forced to juggle and jink his way through the Bolton defence like a panicking shoplifter on the run from security guards. His consummate finish was greeted with astonishment, relief and delight in equal measure.

The semi-final was 135 minutes old and the score was 4-4.

Sixty seconds later, the ball was once again in the back of Richard Wright's net and nobody was quite sure how. The decisive act was Alan Johnston's, looping a powerful shot over Wright from twenty-five yards, but exactly how we had got from celebrating Magilton's goal to being behind in the tie for the fifth time was a source of bafflement to everyone. Confusion was quickly becoming a natural state for everyone in the ground.
The next forty or so minutes were the only bit of the entire contest which felt vaguely like a normal football match - the only period which wasn't punctuated by a rapid-fire exchange of goals, penalties and arguments. Bolton's aggressive approach continued, and racked up more bookings than

their manager had stamps on his Greggs loyalty card, but the conventional cup-tie dynamic took hold. Town had chance after chance, but a mixture of strong goalkeeping from Jääskeläinen, a chunky, uncompromising defence, and a few bits of bad luck, gave rise to the creeping sense that Burley's approach was too pure, almost too perfect, to grind down an opponent like this.

Towards the end, with just a few minutes left to redeem yet another season in the second tier, Burley moved one of his centre-halves, Tony Mowbray, up front. Now here's the thing - that's the sort of tactic that never works. It should stand a reasonable chance - big man wins knock-downs, creates chaos in the box - but in practice it's usually a signal to start checking the train times for the journey home. By this stage, the sheer desperation in the home crowd was almost unbearable, other-worldly - not so much an atmosphere as an all-embracing, wordless, screaming frenzy. The ball was once again launched into the box, Burley's team having finally abandoned their footballing principles. Mowbray dutifully won the header, but who's that picking up the loose ball? Is it predatory goal-machine David Johnson? Is it the trusty right foot of captain Holland? Why no. It's Belfast's very own Duracell-bunny-with-wild-eyes-and-scary-teeth, Jim Magilton.

During his Ipswich career, Jim Magilton averaged a goal every 17 games. I'll run that past you again: one goal every 17 games. He wasn't really in the side to score goals: he was there to keep the team's rhythm and create chances for others, but still. The statistics show that it was reasonable to expect him to pop up with a goal about three times per season. Once every three months.

He'd already got two that night. When the ball fell to him on the edge of the box, the collective gasp of anticipation was audible. One touch, then a right-foot shot which spun perfectly, unreachably, past Jääskeläinen and into the corner of the goal. Looking back at the video, it was probably a mis-kick, but there was no such analysis as it hit the net - just a primal scream of ecstasy from about 20,000 delirious Town fans. There are fewer greater, more organic pleasures in life than being part of a crowd which shares in a moment of pure, astonished celebration. When Jim Magilton completed one of history's most unlikely hat-tricks, we hadn't got promoted - we hadn't even won that semi-final - but the sheer glorious impact of Ipswich, our Ipswich, Burley's Ipswich, finally crossing the line that separates the ruthless winners from the noble runners-up, was unbridled excitement.

Bolton had gone into the game with about as much composure as a Tasmanian Devil with anger management issues, but any semblance of discipline evaporated with that equaliser. Before full-time arrived, Whitlow hauled down Stewart and was shown a second yellow card. Going into extra-time with momentum and a numerical advantage: what could possibly go wrong?

Had you asked any Ipswich fan that question at the time, they would have been knowing enough to realise that the answer was "plenty." But in keeping with the tradition-busting tone of the evening, everything continued to go jaw-droppingly right. Four minutes into extra-time, and Barry Knight was putting his over-worked whistle to use once again, pointing to the penalty spot in front of the Churchman's End for the third time that evening.

Sam Allardyce's post-match rant, when it came, was almost as entertaining as the game itself. He railed against the performance of Knight, displaying the sort of arrogance and bad judgement which would later cost him the England job. He claimed persecution, saying that his team's game at Crystal Palace earlier that season had also been ruined by Knight's incompetence. The only problem was that Knight hadn't been in charge of the Palace game. Not that Sam would be distracted by mere facts. Ignoring the evidence which his team's brutal tactics had presented to 21,000 witnesses, he claimed that the three penalties and two red cards which were eventually awarded against his team were a gross injustice.

It's the third of those spot-kicks which best illustrate how Allardyce was raising the bar of self-delusion. Find the highlights on YouTube and look at the replay: Paul Ritchie literally throws David Johnson to the ground. The ball's gone, there's no danger, but, hyped up to the point of momentary insanity, Ritchie grabs Johnson around the waist and flings him onto the turf. The referee's fault for making a bad decision, according to Allardyce. Someone, however, must have instructed Bolton's players to push the aggression so far that they couldn't control it. Who could that have been, Sam? Sam? Oh, he's off, muttering to himself about the unfairness of it all, probably going to seek solace in a pint of wine.

So, here we are. 5-5 on aggregate, Town with everything in their favour, and awarded a penalty. A chance to break out from the shackles of perennial nearly-people, and end four seasons of frustration. No pressure, then. All eyes, as is becoming usual for the evening, are on regular penalty-taker Magilton, who has already scored one and missed one. Magilton's actions are once again decisive, but perhaps unexpected. He immediately hands the ball to left wing-back Jamie Clapham. A deep breath. Clapham appears to be the calmest person in the ground as he chips it home. It's taken 184 minutes of football, eleven goals, countless near-misses and a huge toll on the cardiac health of every Ipswich fan in the ground, but finally we're ahead in the tie.

The wily Dutchman Martijn Reuser was on as a substitute by this point, and a few minutes after Clapham's penalty, he cleverly drew a foul from Robbie Elliott. Who knows whether or not Reuser was aware that Elliott was one of the Bolton players on a yellow card, but by this stage so many of their players had had their names taken that it was a near-statistical certainty that it would lead to a red. Elliott put up some token protests, but seemed almost relieved to be leaving the pitch while his team-mates had to go through the rest of their increasingly weary motions.

We were a goal up against a team of nine, but Town's history in the play-offs meant that nobody would take anything for granted. It took a final, decisive goal from Reuser, having been set up by the unreconstructed persistence of Richard Naylor, to leave us finally feeling ready to celebrate.
The final whistle went and, in all honesty, everything is a bit of a blur from that point. I think that quite a lot of fans ended up on the pitch.

My Favourite Game

I know that somebody found a microphone with which George Burley and the club's chairman, David Sheepshanks, could address the crowd. I remember Burley saying something like "I'll say to you what I've just said to the players. We're not going to Wembley for a day out. We're going there to win."

Reader, we did win. The final itself, a few days later, was quite the heart-stopping occasion too, but after all that we had been through to get there, I'm not sure that anyone really contemplated the idea of defeat. The team did its best to make it hard for themselves, as was their way, but goals from Mowbray, Stewart, Naylor, and Reuser sealed a 4-2 win over Barnsley and - finally - promotion.

It's said that it's better to travel than to arrive. I don't know if that was quite true of Burley's Ipswich and our journey to the Premier League: certainly it was fun, for a while, when we got there. But that four-year epic struggle to get there, with all of its ups and downs, its tantalising moments of joy and its sometimes unbelievable frustrations - that truly was a magnificent thing to be part of. The journey ended triumphantly at Wembley in the bank holiday sunshine, but its real zenith, the moment when the sum of all its crazy parts finally coalesced into an irresistible whole, came on the 17th May 2000, at Portman Road. Like I said - timing. Some things really are worth waiting for.

Gavin Barber

Ipswich Town 5 Bolton Wanderers 3

Division One Play-off Semi-final, 2nd Leg 1999/2000
Attendance: 21,543
Referee: Barry Knight

IPSWICH TOWN

Manager: George Burley

Team: Richard Wright, Gary Croft, Wayne Brown, Tony Mowbray, Mark Venus, Jamie Clapham, Matt Holland, Jim Magilton, James Scowcroft, David Johnson, Marcus Stewart (Subs: Martijn Reuser, Richard Naylor)

Goals: Magilton (18 pen., 49, 90)
            Clapham (94 pen.)
            Reuser (109)

BOLTON WANDERERS

Manager: Sam Alladyce

Team: Jussi Jääskeläinen, Guðni Bergsson, Mike Whitlow, Paul Warhurst, Mark Fish, Paul Ritchie, Michael Johansen, Claus Jensen, Robbie Elliott, Dean Holdsworth, Allan Johnston (Subs: Bo Hansen, Franck Passi, Jimmy Phillips)

Goals: Holdsworth (6, 39)
            Johnston (50)

EIGHT

Ipswich Town 3 Newcastle United 2
Saturday, 11 April 1992
Portman Road

1991/92 had been a strange season at Portman Road. The previous season had ended with Ipswich Town finishing fourteenth in the table - the lowest finish since the late 1950s. Manager John Lyall's transfer policy was publicly stated as a simple mantra - "The right player at the right price." And clearly, in Lyall's opinion there were either no right players, or right prices that summer, as Town started the season without a new face in the squad. In fact, the last players that had been signed by Lyall had arrived in January, both of whom had played for Lyall at West Ham United in the 1980s.

First of all Steve Whitton would sign from Sheffield Wednesday, and then Paul Goddard would arrive on a free transfer from Millwall. Very few people realised at the time that Whitton would become one of the most important players in an unlikely promotion push. Four players would arrive during the season. Steve Palmer's arrival after completing a degree at Cambridge University was unheralded, but he would become an important part of Town's midfield. Loanee John Moncur from Tottenham Hotspur would be solid and unspectacular, and his return to White Hart Lane led to an unlikely run.

The big money signing - Eddie Youds from Everton - would have an unfortunate start. A £250,000 price tag for a player who had barely played a league game may well have raised eyebrows, but when he broke down injured in the fifty-second minute of his debut away at Derby County, it was the start of a blighted career at Portman Road. Youds would have to wait until the next season for his next game, and almost two years for his first real run in the side. In many ways, Youds' Ipswich career could be summed up by the unfortunate own goal he scored in the last game of that run in the 5-1 home defeat by Arsenal. As the ball headed for the Ipswich goal line, Youds tried to clear it, slipped, sat on the ball, and essentially farted the ball slowly over the line. However, the most important signing that season was a familiar face, who arrived on a temporary basis but would become a permanent fixture in the side for the next four seasons, albeit in a new position, from the one that Ipswich fans had been accustomed to seeing him play in.

The Ipswich defence had started off the season in disarray. Record signing Brian Gayle had never settled in Suffolk, and Lyall had agreed that once another club came in for him at the right price, he could leave. Five games into the season Gayle left for Sheffield United, and it would take a while for the Town defence to settle. Normal right back Frank Yallop had struggled for form and had lost his place to youngster Gavin Johnson, and the new centre-half pairing of club captain David Linighan and Tony Humes didn't last long, as three games into their partnership, Humes would succumb to the latest in a long line of injuries - a broken arm away at Newcastle - and would never play for the club again, eventually leaving on transfer deadline day (the last Thursday of March in those days) to sign for Wrexham. Yallop would partner Linighan for the next few games, but with no defensive backup other than the untested Phil Whelan, Lyall needed a new centre-half, and fast.

At the time, Divison Two clubs entered up to three cup competitions. As well as the FA Cup and the League Cup, there was the Full Members Cup. A cup that was only open to Full Members of the League, namely Division One and Division Two sides. As luck would have it, Town would have a fixture in this competition, away at Bristol Rovers, which would give Lyall a chance to try something. With attendances, and interest in the competition low (the League game between the two sides would attract over four times as many fans), it was a risk worth taking. So, Lyall signed a trialist on a short term contract, and gave him a try at centre-half alongside Yallop - Linighan's importance to the side was too much to risk him. Town won 3-1, and the trialist played well. Well enough to partner Linighan in defence for the next League game at home to Oxford United. John Wark had officially returned to Ipswich for his third spell. The team would take a few weeks to settle down, and then, when Ipswich beat Tranmere Rovers 4-0 at Portman Road on the 30th November, the following team would take to the pitch:

1. Craig Forrest

2. Gavin Johnson   5. John Wark   6. David Linighan   3. Neil Thompson

4. Mick Stockwell   8. Steve Palmer   10. Jason Dozzell   7. Simon Milton

9. Steve Whitton   11. Chris Kiwomya

Remarkably, this side would start eighteen of the next twenty games, winning eleven of them, propelling Ipswich to the heart of the promotion race. So settled was the side, that just five players came on as substitutes - David Lowe, Frank Yallop, Romeo Zondervan, Paul Goddard and Glenn Pennyfather - in fact, it would be Pennyfather that would replace Steve Whitton and Neil Thompson as each missed a single game of the run.

By the time of the Newcastle United home game, just three changes would occur. After a home defeat to Watford in March, a fit-again Zondervan and Goddard would replace Palmer and Johnson (Stockwell and Whitton moving back) with Palmer and Johnson dropping to the substitute's bench. Linighan would get injured during the home win over Barnsley, and Whelan would replace him:

1. Craig Forrest

4. Mick Stockwell   5. John Wark   6. Phil Whelan   3. Neil Thompson

9. Steve Whitton   2. Romeo Zondervan   10. Jason Dozzell   7. Simon Milton

8. Paul Goddard   11. Chris Kiwomya

On top of this settled side, Ipswich had lost three of their previous seventeen League games. However young centre-half Whelan would be playing in just his third ever League game and he'd scored a header from a corner in both of his first two games. The first of these was a 2-1 win over Southend United at Roots Hall, and Town had then beaten Wolverhampton Wanderers 2-1 five days before, thanks to a last minute Steve Whitton penalty, after Chris Kiwomya had been fouled. Newcastle United, on the other hand had been having a tricky time.

Osvaldo Ardiles' run as manager had not been as successful as hoped, and when he was sacked on February 5, the Magpies were second from bottom. Three points ahead of bottom-placed Oxford United, and four points adrift of safety. There were rumours in the press that the club could not afford relegation to Division Three, so with sixteen games left to save their season, they needed a hero. Enter Kevin Keegan. Keegan had played for Newcastle for two seasons, including a season that had seen the Magpies win promotion to the top flight, and there had been shock when he announced his retirement at the relatively young age of thirty-three. Keegan had originally stated that he had no interest in coaching or management, but the lure of saving a club that had taken him to their hearts, was too much.

Elsewhere in the division, there were two big stories. First of all were Blackburn Rovers. Owner and steel magnate Jack Walker had taken control of the club in 1991, and had decided to inject a lot of his fortune into the club, with the dream of taking Blackburn Rovers back to the top flight, and as title challengers. Three games into the season, with Rovers having taken one point from three games, Walker would sack manager Don Mackay, and replace him with former Liverpool manager Kenny Dalglish. Dalglish would break the division's transfer record three times that season - left back Alan Wright, from Blackpool (£500,000), centre-half Colin Hendry from Manchester City (£700,000), and Everton striker Mike Newell (£1.1million) would be joined by Aston Villa midfielder Gordon Cowans, Norwich City midfielder Tim Sherwood, and Swindon Town striker Duncan Shearer.

Overall in an attempt to buy their way out of the division, Blackburn would spend £5 million in five months - unprecedented at the time - and were expected to walk the division. At the more unfashionable end of the scale, there was Cambridge United managed by former player, John Beck. Midfielder Beck had signed for the club in 1986, but had been forced to retire through injury in 1989, and following Chris Turner's resignation in January 1990, Beck was appointed manager. In his first eighteen months, Beck had guided Cambridge to the FA Cup quarter-finals, the Division Four play-offs and the Division Three title. The U's were favourites for relegation, but thanks to Beck's innovative and unorthodox methods - he had taken long ball football to a new level than anyone before, subjected his players to buckets of cold water before games, and employed gamesmanship with the opposition, by only providing cold water to the dressing rooms and repositioning the away dugouts, so that they were in a less advantageous position. As a result, Cambridge would end up not just avoiding relegation, or even a relegation battle, but would challenge for a third successive promotion.

Such stories made for a tight promotion race for the inaugural Premier League. In fact, after Ipswich beat Blackburn on 28th December, the table looked like this, with four teams level on points at the top, and just five points separating the top 10 :

Pos	Team	Pld	Pts	GD
1	Cambridge United	22	41	12
2	Blackburn Rovers	23	41	12
3	Ipswich Town	25	41	8
4	Middlesbrough	24	41	8
5	Southend United	25	40	5
6	Leicester City	24	40	3
7	Portsmouth	23	39	8
8	Derby County	23	38	8
9	Swindon Town	23	36	13

| 10 | Charlton Athletic | 24 | 36 | 2 |

Town's run was still in the embryonic stage, but the money behind Blackburn had made them such big favourites amongst the bookmakers that they had stopped taking bets on Rovers winning the title. At this stage, Ipswich were 11-1 to be Second Division Champions. By the time that Ipswich would take on Newcastle at Portman Road, Town would start the day of the game top of the table, seven points clear of second placed Cambridge United, and ten points clear of free-spending Blackburn. Middlesbrough had beaten Tranmere Rovers 2-1 the night before, to close the gap.:

Pos	Team	Pld	Pts	GD
1	Ipswich Town	40	76	21
2	Cambridge United	41	69	18
3	Blackburn Rovers	39	66	17
4	Middlesbrough	39	65	13
5	Derby County	41	65	12
6	Leicester City	40	65	5
7	Charlton Athletic	40	63	5
8	Swindon Town	40	60	13

At the bottom, Newcastle had pulled themselves up to nineteenth in the table, three points clear of relegation, but had played one more game than Oxford United, Brighton & Hove Albion and Plymouth Argyle below them, and local rivals Sunderland had four games in hand, mainly thanks to their FA Cup run, which would see them lose the final to Liverpool.

The day itself was everything that you would want from a football match in spring, when you are top of the League. The weather was great - a nice warm day, with the sun continually shining, and Portman Road was packed. In the post-Taylor report days, Portman Road had its capacity limited to 28,000. As I always did when I attended games at the time, I would stand in the Churchmans' End with my Wolves-supporting father. To brighten the atmosphere even more, the lone voice in the Churchmans' End that would shout "LINIGHAAAAN YOU WANKAAAAAAH!" once a game, would be silenced due his nemesis' injury. Ipswich lined up as stated above:

1. Craig Forrest

4. Mick Stockwell   5. John Wark   6. Phil Whelan   3. Neil Thompson

9. Steve Whitton   2. Romeo Zondervan   10. Jason Dozzell   7. Simon Milton

8. Paul Goddard   11. Chris Kiwomya

Subs: 12. Steve Palmer, 14. Gavin Johnson

Whereas Newcastle lined up as follows:

1. Tommy Wright

2. Ray Ranson   5. Steve Howey   6. Kevin Scott   3. Mark Stimson
7. Lee Clark   11. Kevin Brock   4. Liam O'Brien   10. Kevin Sheedy
          8. Gavin Peacock   9. David Kelly

Subs: 12 Bjørn Kristensen, 14. Mick Quinn

The referee was Alf Buksh from Dollis Hill in London.

At the time, Ipswich would normally play the first half towards the North Stand, which housed both home and away fans, so that both teams would be attacking their own fans at the start of the second half. However, they lost the toss, and Newcastle captain Kevin Scott elected to change ends. The game started as it would be played out - fast paced, high on energy, and end to end football. On eighteen minutes came the first goal, Craig Forrest caught a speculative cross from the right hand side, and threw the ball out to Mick Stockwell, whose pass forward was intercepted by Liam O'Brien. O'Brien's run forward was blocked by Romeo Zondervan and Jason Dozzell, so he played the ball back to Kevin Brock. Brock played the ball out to Lee Clark on the right, with Simon Milton almost intercepting, but slipping as a result. Milton's slip allowed Clark to play the ball between Milton and Thompson, towards Gavin Peacock, who has his back to goal, turned in front of Phil Whelan, and evading Zondervan's late challenge, aimed the ball beyond Forrest, into the top right hand corner of the net in front of the Churchmans' stand. It was a great finish, but not what Town needed at such an early stage in the game. *Ipswich Town 0 Newcastle United 1.*

On thirty-two minutes, Town would win a corner. Because of his goals in the previous two games, a cry of "WHEE-LAN" went up around the ground. Neil Thompson would take one of his corners (described by many as an Exocet missile, due to their accuracy) which went to the far end of the Newcastle box, where Whelan would beat his man in the air, heading the ball across the box, which was cleared as far as O'Brien. O'Brien could only clear to the edge of the area where Paul Goddard rifled the ball towards the net, only for Ray Ranson to block the ball with the combination of his knee and his hand. Referee Alf Buksh's view was obscured by Ranson's back, but after the linesman flagged, Buksh pointed to the spot. Steve Whitton took the resulting penalty, and sent keeper Tommy Wright the wrong way. *Ipswich Town 1 Newcastle United 1.*

Two minutes before half time came the third goal, and one that was a lot more direct. Kevin Sheedy hit a long ball from just outside the centre circle, over the top of the Town defence. Gavin Peacock beat both the Town offside trap, and outpaced both John Wark and the advancing Craig Forrest, reaching the ball first, six yards out, but at an acute angle. Peacock lobbed the ball over a flailing Forrest, and into the net. The Magpies were ahead once more. *Ipswich Town 1 Newcastle United 2.*

Bjørn Kristensen would come on at half time for Ray Ranson in a straight swap, and the second half would begin with the game continuing at the same pace. Ipswich pressed for an equaliser, but failed to break through. So on the hour, Lyall reverted to one of the changes he had made after the Watford home defeat. Gavin Johnson would come on as right back, Mick Stockwell would move forward, and Steve Whitton would join Chris Kiwomya up front. Steve Palmer would also replace Simon Milton. With Jason Dozzell linking well with Kiwomya, and pushing forward as a result, Ipswich were effectively playing 4-3-3. Town had to wait until halfway through the second half for their second equaliser, and it came in a similar manner to their first. Neil Thompson took a corner, and with Phil Whelan poised at the back of the box, John Wark evaded his marker David Kelly, and nipped in ahead of Whelan and powered a header past the helpless Tommy Wright, who had been blocked by teammate Steve Howey. *Ipswich Town 2 Newcastle United 2.*

Three minutes later, Ipswich had their winner. Mick Stockwell played the ball down the Ipswich right to Steve Whitton, who beat Mark Stimson, before laying the ball off to Steve Palmer, who sprinted past Liam O'Brien and Kevin Scott, before playing the ball across the box, past the advancing Tommy Wright, and into the path of Chris Kiwomya who sidefooted the ball into the net from six yards out for his nineteenth goal of the season. *Ipswich Town 3 Newcastle United 2.*

The Magpies would push for an equaliser, but none was forthcoming. Lee Clark would make way for striker Mick Quinn in the closing stages, with Gavin Peacock dropping back, but even with Quinn and David Kelly being supported by the Peacock, they could not equalise. Ipswich had their fifth successive win. Other results that day would see Cambridge lose 2-1 at Wolverhampton Wanderers, Blackburn lose 2-1 at Watford, Derby County draw 2-2 at home to Oxford, with Leicester City being the only team in the top six other than Ipswich to win, as they beat Barnsley 3-1 at Filbert Street. As a result, Ipswich would go 10 points clear of second placed Cambridge, and 11 points clear of third placed Leicester:

Pos	Team	Pld	Pts	GD
1	Ipswich Town	41	79	22
2	Cambridge United	42	69	17
3	Leicester City	41	68	7
4	Blackburn Rovers	40	66	16
5	Derby County	42	66	12
6	Charlton Athletic	41	66	6
7	Middlesbrough	39	65	13

Just five points would be needed to see Ipswich gain promotion back to the top flight, and the newly-created Premier League, and six points would see them crowned champions. At the bottom, just two of Newcastle's rivals would pick up points - as well as Oxford - draw at Derby, Port Vale would come off the bottom with a 2-1 win over Brighton. The next few weeks would be nervy. Ipswich would lose successive games at Sunderland and Bristol City, and with a win needed at home to Grimsby to seal promotion, a frustrating goalless draw meant that Town still needed points to get over the line. By now, Leicester had cut the lead to three points, Derby County and Middlesbrough were also closing, Cambridge were starting to fade, but were hanging in there, but with one point from three games, Blackburn had gone from looking to sneak automatic promotion, to dropping out of the playoff places:

Pos	Team	Pld	Pts	GD
1	Ipswich Town	44	80	18
2	Leicester City	44	77	10
3	Derby County	44	72	16
4	Middlesbrough	43	71	13
5	Cambridge United	44	70	16
6	Charlton Athletic	43	68	6
7	Blackburn Rovers	43	67	14
8	Swindon Town	43	65	14
9	Portsmouth	42	65	14

At the bottom, two further defeats to Millwall and Derby had seen Newcastle drop into the bottom six, and with Leicester and Portsmouth to come, their run-in looked bleak. Saturday, 25th April would prove pivotal. With Leicester losing 2-0 to Charlton, all Ipswich needed to win not just promotion, but the Second Division Championship, was a point at the Manor Ground, and a 1-1 draw, with a goal courtesy of a ninth minute

Gavin Johnson equaliser to an early Oxford goal scored by future Ipswich player and manager Jim Magilton would see Ipswich promoted back to the top flight as champions. Newcastle would beat both Leicester and Portsmouth, and finish four points clear of safety, only to follow Town as champions twelve months later. Leicester's last minute stumble, would see Middlesbrough sneak into runners-up place, while Blackburn would turn their late season form around in time to sneak into sixth place, and the play-offs, and would win the final against Leicester City thanks to a late penalty won with an outrageous dive by David Speedie.

FINAL TABLE:

Pos	Team	Pld	Pts	GD
1	Ipswich Town	46	84	20
2	Middlesbrough	46	80	17
3	Derby County	46	78	18
4	Leicester City	46	77	7
5	Cambridge United	46	74	18
6	Blackburn Rovers	46	74	17
7	Charlton Athletic	46	71	6

Over the summer, Portman Road would be one of two top flight stadia converted to all-seater, along with Norwich City's Carrow Road. Portman Road's capacity would be reduced to just over 22,500 as a result. The conversion was done in secret, with the announcement only coming after work would be completed. Not for the first, or last time, the management at Ipswich Town would know how to take the shine off optimism at Portman Road with an unpopular decision.

Rob Freeman

Ipswich Town 3 Newcastle United 2
Division Two 1991/92
Attendance: 20,649
Referee: Alf N. Buksh

IPSWICH TOWN

Manager: John Lyall

Team: Craig Forrest, Romeo Zondervan, Neil
Thompson, Mick Stockwell, John Wark, Phil Whelan, Simon
Milton, Paul Goddard, Steve Whitton, Jason Dozzell, Chris
Kiwomya (Subs: Gavin Johnson, Steve Palmer)

Goals: Whitton (32 pen.)
             Wark (69)
             Kiwomya (72)

NEWCASTLE UNITED

Manager: Kevin Keegan

Team: Tommy Wright, Ray Ranson, Mark
Stimson, Liam O'Brien, Kevin Scott, Steve Howey, Lee Clark,
Gavin Peacock, David Kelly, Kevin Sheedy, Kevin Brock (Subs:
Mick Quinn, Bjørn Kristensen)

Goals: Peacock (17, 42)

NINE

Ipswich Town 1 Inter Milan 0
Thursday, 22 November 2001
Portman Road

There are occasions that you remember purely because of what they were, rather than because they were particularly brilliant or wonderful. Going to see the Ramones was like that. I don't remember too much about it - it was a very long time ago - but I do remember that I wore the brand new pair of size three cherry red Doctor Martens that I'd bought earlier the same afternoon, although I couldn't name a single song that the Ramones played, or even if they were particularly good that night. Of course the detail doesn't really matter as much as the fact that I was there and at the time I thought that it was the coolest thing ever. I still do.

The match when we beat Inter Milan at Portman Road falls into this hazy category too. It certainly wasn't the greatest football match I've ever seen. It wasn't even the greatest game I saw that season, I'm sure. But some things just stay with you. And remembering them, momentarily going back to another time and place so long ago, also means remembering all the things that have changed in your life since that moment. So many things have changed for me since then: I've moved house, I've changed career, some people have gone out of my life and others have come into it, several dearly loved people have gone forever. Through all this, there has been only one constant, running through the years like a bright blue thread in my life's fabric. That thread is Ipswich Town Football Club.

*

I was standing up in the south corner of the Cobbold Stand at Portman Road in one of the sections that are usually reserved for away fans. That afternoon I had travelled down from North Norfolk by train, dropped my bag off at my in-laws' house and enjoyed the considerable pleasures of Ipswich's pubs. The ground was filling up, the game was about to begin, the atmosphere was excited, anticipatory, tense.

Next to me, separated by a few empty seats, were several hundred away supporters and among them, about two yards away from me, was one Intermilan fan in particular. I'd already noticed him in town earlier, because, well, he stood out a bit in Princes Street. He was certainly every English fan's stereotypical idea of an Italian *ultra*, with his slicked, coal black hair, his floor-length black leather trench coat - all his clothes were black - and his slightly aggressive stance. He was quite tiny too: wiry, thin and not very tall. If Barbie's boyfriend Ken had gone through a neo-Nazi phase, he would have looked like this guy. (Ken's sporting a man-bun nowadays, by the way.) I wondered if the *ultra* was a Fascist of some kind. He looked like my idea of one - the Italian version, of course, not the kind of overweight skinhead who used to sell *National Front News* in the marketplace at Bury St Edmunds - and he had a pugnacious demeanour, and all in all was not unlike a very short Paolo di Canio. I made a mental note to check Google for information about the complicated politics of Serie A clubs when I got home.

This guy looked a little bit lost at Portman Road. A pocket-sized *ultra*, a deadly lanternshark that had lost its way, straying into the floodlit pool of our massive blue and white arena and suddenly becoming aware that - far from being its snappily-dressed kingpin - he was an alien in a world that really didn't belong to him. He didn't seem very happy, even before the match had begun. By the time the referee blew the final whistle, he would be furious.

*

My childhood interest in football was firmly quashed when, despite my feeble protests, I was made to spend Saturday afternoons shopping with my mother while my brother went to the match with Dad and my uncle. I often mention this, not because it's a preamble to a feminist diatribe about discrimination but because it's the beginning of a story with a much happier ending called How I was Saved From the Terrible Fate of Becoming a Stoke City Supporter. Or The Great Escape. Far from feeling resentful about it, or puzzling over how the vagaries of my life have led me to Suffolk and to Portman Road, I am forever grateful.

Hardly a star schoolgirl athlete myself - yes, I was that person who was left out after the teams had been picked and I was frequently sent to play tennis on my own, a strange and humiliating experience to say the least.

Having been so comprehensively discouraged, most sport took a back seat in my life for many years while music took over in a big way. For a very long time, football was something that I was indifferent to and I missed out on many great and famous Ipswich Town occasions because of that. On the other hand, I also missed the John Duncan years.

The re-kindling of my passion for football did not come from a visit to Portman Road however. At least, not at first. It came from that much-maligned method of enjoying the game, watching football on television. I was unwell during most of the 1990s and for several years I was unable to walk very far. Suddenly, one of the greatest pleasures in my life was watching football - and watching one television programme in particular - *Football Italia* on Channel 4. I fell for the whole thing, hook, line and *semifreddo*. If you wanted drama on television in the 1990s, there was *Brookside*, *Ballykissangel* and *The Bill* - or there was Batigol.

Players like Gattuso and Batistuta looked - and often behaved - as if they'd escaped from a seventeenth-century revenge tragedy. If the players had come onto the pitch wearing doublets and carrying stilettos (I mean knives, not the shoes) I would not have been surprised. They played in colours like raspberry and orange (Roma), black and red stripes (AC Milan) and violet - Fiorentina were my favourites from the beginning, and they still are, despite their best efforts to put me off. Don't ask me to discuss the role of the *libero*, or *catenaccio*, for me *calcio* is all about theatre. And it was not just the players who were part of the drama: there were referees like Pierluigi Collina, managers like Fabio Capello, Lippi with his cigars, and Ancelotti - who always seemed to be sitting in the stands in front of Berlusconi's sinister-looking henchman with a terrified expression on his face. Giovanni Trapattoni appeared to have wandered into the San Siro from an Abruzzese version of *One Man and his Dog*. And then there was the programme's presenter, James Richardson, with his manic chirpyness, madly waving copies of the latest issue of *Corriere dello Sport*, while sitting outside a caffè in the Italian sunshine, drinking coffee and waiting for the arrival of his latest, increasingly supersized and baroque, dessert of the day. Even without any football, *Football Italia* was the best thing on TV.

From *omertà* to early doors. I soon learned that the world of *Football Italia* was not the real world of football. It was a far cry from watching Steve Whitton's Colchester United playing at the Britannia Stadium, or even a cold, grey Saturday afternoon at Portman Road. It seemed to me that it was conducted in a parallel universe where everything was better, funnier, sunnier and more glamorous. The very thought of seeing some of these players walking onto the pitch at my home ground meant that something strange in the order of the universe must have happened. The odd looking half-timbered building above the tunnel from where the players came out might be a weird fissure in time and space for all I knew. I couldn't wait to see these players in the flesh and it never occurred to me for a moment before the game started that Héctor Cúper would not put out a full strength side.

I was probably more familiar with the background of the Inter squad than I was with our usual opponents in the Premier League, a promised land we had only just arrived at in May 2000, via the Championship play-offs. Town, of course, had its own Italian connections at this time, with Matteo Sereni in goal and Inter's own Sixto Peralta on loan to us. The television commentator that night mentioned this when the camera showed Sixto limbering up, exclaiming - so ominously that it was comical - "So they'll know ALL about him!"

Ready to Go by Republica, *Right Here, Right Now* by Fat Boy Slim. The players came out of the tunnel. (I'm guessing that those were the tunes, and I bet I'm right.)

The programme promised great things but a cold waft of reality hit me like a North Sea gale in February and I finally realised that Inter would not risk their biggest stars on this cold Thursday night in East Anglia. To my great disappointment, Sérgio Conceiçao was only on the bench. There was no Ronaldo at all, no Vieri and no Recoba, all players that I'd admired hugely, so it was beginning to feel like a real let-down. But despite that, this second-string Inter Milan team still boasted the talents of Emre Belözoglu, Di Biagio, the great *custode del sacchetto di cipolla* Toldo, Clarence Seedorf, Cristiano Zanetti, and to my delight, I would have the pleasure - no, the honour - of watching one of my all-time favourite footballers play on my club's home ground.

Javier Zanetti. Nicknames: *Il Capitano* and *El tractor*. No, really.

Javier Zanetti. Among all those loathsome Argentinians, here was someone you could admire, and with that haircut, even your dad might like him.

Javier Zanetti. The man who took a pair of trainers to his own wedding.

Then there's his politics. Born in one of the poorest districts of Buenos Aires, he is more politically aware than your average full back and has done a great deal for children's charities in both Italy and his native Argentina. He once managed to persuade his teammates in Milan to donate money for the Mexican revolutionary movement, the Zapatistas. To raise money, they were fined for being late or using their mobile phones at inappropriate times. In his autobiography he explained his reasons for supporting them: "Solidarity knows no colour, no religion and no political side. These communities fight to make their culture recognized as well as a different way of economical and political organization, of surviving and of identity."

Zanetti would probably have been one of my favourite footballers just for writing that, regardless of the fact that he was one of the greatest of all defenders (even Jose Mourinho agrees with me, having picked him for his all-time XI, although he played him as a midfielder when he was the manager of Inter). His longevity (nineteen years at the San Siro), the number of trophies that he won, and the hard work that enabled him to overcome his shortcomings as a player are all cited as aspects of his greatness but can also be held against him. The dullness of a one-club player, who was also a one-hairstyle player, a man who did nothing to get himself in the gossip columns, who has been described as a Ford compared to Maicon's Maserati. Who cares? Cars are boring. This man was quietly, unobtrusively, always there, passing the ball with heft and grace, always perfect, wherever he was asked to play. Give me that rather than the self-aggrandising antics of an Ibramovich or a Balotelli any day.

When Zanetti finally retired at the age of forty, tributes were paid to him by players and coaches all over the world. It's interesting that even they found it difficult to describe him as a player. Phrases like "serene grit and determination" had to suffice, along with references to his dignity, his constant presence in the team. At times the praise took on an almost religious, mystical aspect. His friend and teammate Cambiasso simply said: "He is supernatural."

And there he was. On Mr. Ferguson's gorgeous green turf at Portman Road.

Sadly, neither Javier Zanetti nor the match itself turned out to be as great as I'd hoped. George Burley had dropped Martijn Reuser - a player guaranteed to live up to a special occasion - and replaced him with Jamie Clapham, who hadn't played for a while. Jermaine Wright came in for Jim Magilton who was injured and Richard Naylor was playing up front, instead of our young star, Darren Bent. None of the chosen players were bad footballers, but it hardly promised to be Ipswich at its stylish best. The

Italians did not appear to be enjoying the cold weather and were clearly going to be happy to go home with a nil-nil draw.

Nevertheless, Titus Bramble gave us some unexpected early excitement when he came close to scoring. At the other end, only a brilliant save by Sereni prevented Nicola Ventola from putting the ball into the net. Soon afterwards, Ventola was brought down right in front of the goal. If the ref had been Andy D'Urso, it would have been a penalty. Thankfully, it was Kim Nielsen - another figure pleasingly teleported in from the world of televised international football.

Richard Naylor could still do no wrong in my eyes. His performance in the play-off final against Barnsley was so magnificent, that it rarely occurred to me to question why George Burley would play a defender as a striker. A defender, it might be added, probably in capital letters, WHOSE KNEES WERE COMPLETELY KNACKERED. So I was annoyed when he was replaced by Alun Armstrong in the seventy-seventh minute. Armstrong had been "suffering from a virus" for weeks and besides, he had never really caught my attention as a forward like Pablo or Reuser or.... Richard Naylor. At that moment, Burley's decision almost felt like capitulation.

The goal, when it came, only a few minutes later, was the result of a lovely move from Couñago, who seemed to be everywhere that night, but whose finishing had been disastrous ("Oh for a greedy striker!" the commentator complained on the match highlights, watching an earlier example of Pablo's game: an unselfish pass to Peralta when he should have taken a shot on goal himself), and there wouldn't have been a goal at all, had it not been for a sublime cross into the box from Jamie Clapham. A climbing Armstrong headed it into the net, leaving Toldo flapping around in his goalmouth. And so, because of this one magnificent moment, it is Alun Armstrong, of Stockport County, Middlesbrough and Ipswich Town, who earned the right to forever be able to tell his grandchildren, or anyone else who cares to listen, of how he scored the winning goal against Internazionale, under the lights at Portman Road one Thursday night in November, long ago.

Armstrong scored in the eighty-first minute and I knew that it was the winning goal as soon as it went in, despite the fact that Inter Milan were a much better attacking side than we were. The remaining minutes didn't drag like they had at several play-off games in recent memory, nor did I feel horribly sick as I had for the entire second half of the promotion play-off final at Wembley. It simply seemed right. I have never felt quite the same way about my team as I did about George Burley's side in that period of the club's history. They were by no means the best players we'd ever had, either individually or collectively, but there was something about them that was very special indeed

It was not a particularly good game of football. It stands out for me because I was there, privileged to watch my team play one of the great sides of the world, and to not merely be equal to the task, but to come away as the deserved winners. I think the reason why this is such a strong memory is that it felt perfectly right for us, for Ipswich Town, to be there, playing with, and equal to, the great teams and the greatest players in Europe. It was then that I knew that this was our rightful place in football, playing on the international stage, the universally-admired offspring of two brilliant fathers, Alf Ramsey and Bobby Robson. A club that did things the right way, that had the right values, that represented something good in the often justifiably maligned world of professional football.

I wonder if it will ever happen again and I doubt it somehow. But it happened that night. I was there and I wasn't dreaming.

*

We scurried to the Plough to celebrate with a few pints before getting the bus back to my in-laws' house and to my great shame, at about twenty past eleven, I rang my brother in Carlisle to tell him the Glorious News. To be fair to him, a Stoke City fan who had two babies sleeping upstairs at the time (both of whom I had temporarily forgotten about, bad auntie that I was), he didn't sound the least bit annoyed as I drunkenly babbled on about Pablo, Sixto, Armstrong and Zanetti - but then he loves football too, so I like to think he understood.

The next morning, dragging myself and my hangover to Ipswich station to catch the train back to Cromer, I saw the *ultra* again, still dressed in his long, black leather coat, but wearing black Raybans to hide his eyes from the bright Suffolk morning sun, looking even more incongruous in the somewhat prosaic and orange surroundings of the Upper Crust railway buffet.

He was still complaining.

Susan Gardiner

Ipswich Town 1 Inter Milan 0
UEFA Cup, Third Round, First Leg, 2001/2
Attendance: 24,569
Referee: Kim Nielsen

IPSWICH TOWN

Manager: George Burley

Team: Matteo Sereni, Chris Makin, Titus Bramble, Herman Hreiðarsson, Mark Venus, Jermaine Wright, Matt Holland, Sixto Peralta, Jamie Clapham, Pablo Couñago, Richard Naylor. (Subs: Martijn Reuser, Thomas Gaardsøe, Alun Armstrong)

Goals: Armstrong (82)

INTER MILAN

Manager: Héctor Cúper

Team: Francesco Toldo, Javier Zanetti, Iván Córdoba, Luigi Di Biagio, Vratislav Greško, Clarence Seedorf, Cristiano Zanetti, Emre Belözoglu, Javier Farinós, Mohamed Kallon, Nicola Ventola. (Subs: Grigorios Georgatos, Sérgio Conceição, Adriano)

TEN

Ipswich Town 3 Crewe Alexandra 2
Sunday, 3 May 1998
Portman Road

Who are the supporters which a club can count on, come rain or shine? Are they the supporters who turn up on a drab winter evening for a match against unglamorous opposition? On Tuesday, 4th November 1997, just 8,938 loyal souls rattled around Portman Road for a match against Stockport County. These are what most people consider to be the club's core fanbase.

For me though, the supporters which a club can count on are the ones who come for the social side of things, for the match as an event, and for the atmosphere. And there's no better time to observe them in their natural habitat than at the Meaningless Last Match Of The Season.

You know the situation. Nothing's going to happen. Two teams whose position in the final table is assured, simply there for a kickaround which will fulfil their obligations to the league. Players, management and supporters with one thing in common - their minds are elsewhere. It might be the beach, it might be the play-offs, or it might be next August. Whatever the case, nobody in the ground will be "giving it 110%" except maybe the barman in Legends.

Yet still we come. And another thing about the Meaningless Last Match Of The Season: it's always sunny. Met Office records suggest that the weather on a Saturday afternoon at the start of May is quite likely to be as drab as George Graham's first season at Leeds. But I don't remember ever needing anything other than shirtsleeves.

My favourite Meaningless Last Match Of The Season comes from 1998. It illustrates perfectly the hold which our club has over us. But first, a digression.

Throughout the 1990s, my employer did business with a division of

Panasonic, based in Milton Keynes. These were the days when sales and marketing departments were copiously funded, and offering corporate hospitality was almost compulsory. Panasonic had an 'executive box' at Arsenal's old Highbury Stadium, before the club decamped up the road, and I was lucky enough to be invited on several occasions.

The company's executive box hosted about a dozen people, but the remarkable aspect was that the boxes either side had clearly been allocated to Arsenal Football Club itself. Glance to the left, and you'd see Mrs Bergkamp and assorted children. To the right, celebrity fans like David Frost, hosted by the likes of Charlie George.

On one visit, I asked how the company had managed to be given that particular executive box. Now, this is probably an apocryphal tale, but they explained that they'd approached the club the year before about having a box for a season, and had been laughed out of court. It turned out that the waiting list was about twenty years into the future. As the company was about to strike out that particular corporate hospitality option, someone in the office remarked: "You know who sponsors Arsenal, don't you?"

"Yeah, JVC."

"And you know who owns JVC?"

A few phone calls later, Arsenal had magically found Panasonic, the owners of JVC, another executive box. I'm not sure which club guests had to give up their prized seats, but in the end, it's all about the sponsors.

I have to say, it's a great way to watch football. So when I was asked if I wanted to come up to Highbury as a guest to watch Arsenal play Everton, I was delighted.

Then I looked at my calendar.

Infuriatingly, Ipswich were at home that same afternoon. What's more, it was the Meaningless Last Match Of The Season. I couldn't possibly miss watching my own team, even if the alternative was a Premiership match. You'll understand, I'm sure.

I politely apologised and said that I wouldn't be able to attend.

Almost as soon as I put the phone down, I began to have doubts about what I'd instinctively done. It had been another good season for Ipswich, under George Burley, with the playoffs assured for a second year running. So it wasn't really the last match, because there were the playoffs still to come. But meaningless it was.

Town were bizarrely marooned in fifth place, seven points behind Charlton and six points ahead of Sheffield United. The only thing that mattered in the final regular league game was that nobody got injured or dismissed, so we were hardly likely to see total commitment from our lads.

And the opponents? Not exactly unmissable. With no due respect, a Crewe Alexandra team which was solidly mid-table was hardly box office gold.

Things got worse. I forgot to mention that Arsenal were four points clear at the top of the Premiership, with three games to play. Challengers Manchester United only had two left, so an Arsenal win against Everton would crown them champions. Football had of course only been invented five years before, and this would be the first time the Premiership title would have gone outside Manchester or, er, Blackburn.

It might be quite the party that Saturday at Highbury. I wouldn't be there, however.

In the days leading up to the two matches, the newspapers and TV got quite animated about the prospect of the Premiership trophy coming to London. We had to console ourselves with a bit of email chat on Andrew Young's Ipswich Town supporters' mailing list. That was more than most clubs had. We also had a website, run at different times by Phil Clarke, Paul Felton and Martyn Amos. It had been the first in English football, maybe even the world, but it wasn't the sort of interactive extravaganza we take for granted today. Social media was ten years in the future. You kids don't know you're born.

I was consoled that the match against Crewe should be fun. Well, the afternoon's experience should be, anyway. Town were playing bright, attractive football and the atmosphere around Portman Road was good. The season had seen a couple of notable introductions to the squad, the most significant being Matt Holland, who became my favourite ever Ipswich player and remains so to this day, after nearly fifty years as a supporter. Then in November, with Town in the relegation zone, the club saw the arrival of the relatively unknown David Johnson, who had already scored eight goals for Bury a few places higher up the table. Johnson would score a further twenty-two for Town that year.

1997/98 had provided plenty of talking points and memorable moments. A fine Coca-Cola Cup run began with the first of an incredible six matches that season against Charlton Athletic. The campaign only ended in the quarter-finals after a penalty shoot-out with Chelsea. Solidly in the bottom half of the table at new year, Town would then go on a sixteen-match unbeaten run in reaching the play-offs with ease. New coach Bryan Hamilton was instrumental in this.

February had seen the team score five goals at Portman Road on an incredible three occasions, against Huddersfield, Oxford and most memorably Norwich. The first half hat-trick in the local derby sealed Alex Mathie's place in Suffolk history. However, the Oxford game was just as memorable, as poor Matt Holland ended up in goal after Richard Wright took a blow to the face. Of all the matches for this to happen, Holland got the one where the opposition had a six-foot seven-inch centre forward, Kevin Francis, who scored.

Some long-term features of Portman Road life had also made their debuts this season: the first use of the term "Tractor Boys", and the famous Matt Holland and Jason Cundy "lap of appreciation" at the end of each match. For me, a highlight had been seeing my seven-year-old nephew lead the team out in the home match against Tranmere. I've often pointed to the photograph on my wall of the tiny mascot with the two captains and asked people: "What's wrong with this?" Look carefully and you'll see that Tony Mowbray's opponent has an Ipswich badge on his shirt. The referee had objected to Tranmere's white strip, and the only solution was for Town to offer the visitors a set of their red training tops.

So here we were in May, in good spirits, for the last match of the regular season. Over 19,000 supporters filled Portman Road, despite the irrelevance of the fixture. Town's starting line-up included season ever-presents Richard Wright, Mick Stockwell and Matt Holland, and was the same side as would play against Charlton in the first play-off tie the following Saturday. The idea of resting players was clearly not something which interested George Burley.

The remainder of the team was Mauricio Taricco, Kieron Dyer, Mark Venus, Jason Cundy, Jamie Clapham, David Johnson, Alex Mathie and Bobby Petta. For me, it was probably the best Town squad since Bobby Robson left. Nine of the starting eleven would play in most of the matches the following season, and half of them would form the core of the side which eventually gained promotion to the Premiership two years later. On the bench were James Scowcroft, Danny Sonner and Gus Uhlenbeek, all three of them entertainers in their own right. Scowie had experienced run-ins with some unappreciative home fans that season. They were wrong in their assessment of him. In so many seasons since, we've missed having a striker with that much presence and ability.

The fans were pleased to see both Ipswich and Crewe attacking from the start. David Johnson missed an early chance (was it me, or did he always miss as many as he scored?). Just after the half-hour Johnson made it 1-0 (see?) but before half time, Town had conceded a soft equaliser. Nobody really cared.

As an interesting footnote, although we had no idea at the time, Crewe had two players on show who would go on to have significant Town careers. A year later Jermaine Wright would be signed to replace Kieron Dyer, and some ten years later David Wright (no relation) would become one of the most reliable right backs to play for Ipswich for many years.

After the break, Town won a penalty but Kieron Dyer put it well wide. Nobody seemed to worry that much. The North Stand was having too much fun with the Crewe keeper, who was enjoying himself in return. Then in a frantic ten minute period, Town scored a second through Stockwell and a third through Mathie, before conceding the goal of the game, a screamer by Crewe's Steve Garvey. Exhibition stuff. Almost enough to make me forget what might have been going on at Highbury. Almost.

Down in north London, Arsenal had gone three goals up and the title was all but theirs. If the home fans were having a giggle at Portman Road, those at Highbury were having a real party. It couldn't get better than this, could it? Yes it could. If any footage of the Ipswich v Crewe match still exists, I doubt that anyone has seen it for years. But in the last minute of the Arsenal v Everton match came a moment which remains a Sky Sports archive staple to this very day.

You know what happened. Everton lost possession on the halfway line. As players stood poised, awaiting the outcome of the midfield scramble, Arsenal captain Tony Adams sprinted from the back, right through all of them, towards the Everton goal. Even now, after we've seen it a hundred times, it remains an amazing move. Steve Bould chipped the ball over everyone for it to fall perfectly in front of Adams, who had nobody near him and just the keeper to beat. Adams chested it down and planted it in the corner of the net. That's Tony Adams, of all people. You don't have to be an Arsenal fan to find it incredible to watch, even today.

Back at Portman Road, I expect we were applauding our players off, and looking forward to the upcoming play-offs for the second season running. Sure, it was the Meaningless Last Match Of The Season. But you had to be there.

Chris Rand

Ipswich Town 3 Crewe Alexandra 2
Division One 1997/98
Attendance: 19,105
Referee: Roger Furnandiz

IPSWICH TOWN

Manager: George Burley

Team: Richard Wright, Mick Stockwell, Mauricio Taricco, Kieron Dyer, Mark Venus, Jason Cundy, Jamie Clapham, Matt Holland, David Johnson, Alex Mathie, Bobby Petta (Subs: James Scowcroft, Danny Sonner, Gus Uhlenbeek)

Goals: Johnson (33)
                Stockwell (53)
                Mathie (54)

CREWE ALEXANDRA

Manager: Dario Gradi

Team: Ade Bankole, Shaun Smith, Marcus Bignot, Mark Foran, Lee Unsworth, Phil Charnock, Steve Garvey, Kenny Lunt, Peter Smith, Seth Johnson, Steve Anthrobus (Subs: Mark Rivers, David Wright, Jermaine Wright)

Goals: Charnock (40)
                Garvey (59)

ELEVEN

Watford 0 Ipswich Town 1
Saturday, 21 March 2015
Vicarage Road

Why do we go to football? For me, the answer is relatively simple: a
sense of belonging. Growing up, I was a huge tomboy, heavily influenced by
my mum, who is a former PE teacher and I used to play as much sport as
was going. I enjoyed playing cricket, netball and tennis but I loved playing
football the most. It never occurred to me to actually watch it though. This
all changed during the 1998 World Cup, when England played Argentina in
the knockout stages. Being young and inexperienced with regards to England
in international tournaments, a Shearer equaliser caused me and my brother
to excitedly create England flags out of sticky labels with "SHEARER" em-
blazoned on them and stick them around the house. Needless to say, Beckham's sending off and England's eventual loss on penalties caused them to
very quickly come down again the next morning.

After that, I spent a lot of time in the tiny library at my primary school
reading about the great game. I didn't yet have a football team to support.
My brother found a tiny book listing pages and pages of football statistics
and I, intrigued, flicked through, desperate to know more about this game.
I discovered that a side called Preston North End had once beaten a side
26-0. I excitedly told my brother that we should support them because they
seemed quite good, but he pointed out that Preston's victory had been in the
1880s, rather than the 1980s. Like most Generation Premiership children, I
briefly pondered the idea of supporting Manchester United. David Beckham,
despite kicking Diego Simeone, was still much loved, but thankfully, this
didn't come to pass. One day, in early 2000, my dad came home from work
and announced that he'd got the family tickets to go and watch a local side
play: Ipswich Town Football Club. It was at home game against Hudders-

field Town in February, Marcus Stewart's home debut. Ipswich won 2-1, with Stewart scoring against the side he'd recently departed. We sat behind the dugout, with me getting freshly electronically-tagged Gary Croft's autograph.

I found an old diary where I'd written that the entire occasion had been a "great honour." Ever since that game, I've been hooked. Football became my escape and the only thing I would talk about. Suddenly I knew utterly useless facts, like when Tony Mowbray's birthday was and what Matt Holland's wife was called. I absorbed information like a sponge, being able to tell anyone who made the mistake of listening just what Marcus Stewart had done that weekend. I missed the Wembley glory of 2000 due to a village Street Fair, which my dad helped to organise, but I remember sitting in the pub (owned by Norwich City fans) with my family after the conclusion of the fair. Ipswich fans arrived back from Wembley, beeping their horns as they drove into the pub car park with scarves flying out of their windows.

After a season on the ballot for Premier League tickets, we became season ticket holders up in the gods of the Britannia Stand for the relegation season. Even that disappointment couldn't staunch the passion those eleven men in blue and white inspired within me. Our season ticket moved from the gods into the family section next to the tunnel and we continued our bi-weekly trips to Portman Road as a family, with occasional away trips, right up until my brother went to university in 2008. Our four became a three and, as I entered my first year of sixth form, I decided that it was time for me to start going to football by myself. I still had my season ticket with my parents, but I wanted to venture further afield and, as my mum and dad didn't really fancy trips to some of the more glamorous towns of England, I entered the world of the official supporters' coach. My first solo away game was a 0-0 draw against Sheffield Wednesday. It was a few days after my seventeenth birthday in 2008. Friends asked me what I was going to do to mark the momentous occasion and seemed bemused that I'd rather go to Sheffield than throw a party. My main memory of the day is that I had an absolutely stinking cold. I went through more packets of tissues than Ipswich had shots on goal. I continued to head to away games, occasionally being joined by my parents (my mum has never forgiven me for a long coach trip to Doncaster) or the odd friend who I managed to persuade with the promise of chocolate on the bus rather than on-pitch entertainment. They very rarely joined me again. In 2010, I had to give up my season ticket as well, as I started studying at Lancaster University. My trips to Portman Road became restricted to holidays although my solo away trips continued. Given my location in the north-west, I soon racked up the grounds, spending afternoons and evenings in Blackburn, Burnley and at various locations across the Pennines. Ironically, it was only after I graduated that I managed to get to Blackpool, one of easiest away days for a Lancaster student. During these northern away days, I began to meet people through social media, or in away stands up and down the country, and regularly met up with them in football pubs or at the ground. I graduated in 2013. For the 2013/14 season, my trips to Portman Road were few and far between. I took on work at local libraries and disappeared off to Australia for five weeks to watch England get stuffed in the Ashes. It was when I returned, and a few months after McCarthy had taken over, that I, after much umming and ahhing over post-university finances, decided to return to Portman Road for the 2014/15 season. My parents had given up their season tickets during my time at university; the enjoyment had gone and they didn't see the point in forking out a small fortune to watch us play terribly every other weekend. So, I ended up getting a season ticket on my own in the place I'd always wanted to be as a child: the North Stand.

During this time, my brother had moved to Brussels for work and had drifted somewhat from following Town. As I made my way across the north, blindly supporting whatever rubbish was served up in front of me, distance and Town's continued mediocrity dulled my brother's interest in the game. It was only the thrills and spills of the Belgian Third Division football (our 2016/17 pre-season opponents of Royale Union Saint-Gilloise were his side) that reminded my brother of the joy of football. When he moved back to the UK in 2014, buoyed by the McCarthy appointment and a 2-1 win over Sheffield Wednesday at the end of the 2013/14 season we'd attended, he decided that he wanted to start going to London away games. We found ourselves going to Charlton (Noel Hunt and Luke Chambers' infamous post-match interview) and then onto Fulham (Daryl Murphy's Venetian mask). QPR and Reading followed, although we'd not yet made it to Brentford. So, why Watford away? Of all the games I could've picked, why this one? Why not the 6-4 against Crewe or the 5-0 versus Sunderland? Why not the 3-2 against Norwich or even the 2-2 against West Ham, despite everything that followed?

2014/15 was the season that Ipswich, after ten very long, tedious years, finally made it back into the play-offs and, for me, two matches stand out. Both were against Watford. Both, I went to with my brother. The fixture at Portman Road in November 2014 was a bad-tempered affair, with Jonny Williams suffering a thigh injury after a nasty tackle from Joel Ekstrand. Whilst bad-tempered, it was also a fairly decent match with two evenly matched sides, trying to break through two stubborn defences and up against two goalkeepers in top form. It was fitting that the winner was scored by a defender. When Tommy Smith managed to poke the ball into the back of the net, the home end erupted. We had beaten a top six opponent and had played well whilst doing so. We move on to March 2015. Ipswich's recent record at Vicarage Road hadn't been great until a last-minute Michael Chopra goal had broken the hoodoo back in 2012. Our form leading up to our 2014/15 visit to Watford had also been poor (which is standard for the second half of a McCarthy season) and we had slipped from second in the league to seventh, while Watford had climbed to the top. So, why is this my favourite game? To go back to my earlier question, why do we go to football?

Football brings groups of individuals together in a united cause. Nearly every Saturday, with the occasional Sunday and Tuesday thrown in, individuals put on a football shirt and become part of a community. You might be at the ground, you might be in the supermarket, you might be halfway up a mountain in Peru. As long as you are wearing that shirt, you are a part of that community: you chant, together; you experience an agonising shot past the post, together; you call the referee a wanker, together. Watford away captured that spirit perfectly. It was another Inflatables Day. Chris Kamara, reporting for Soccer Special, watched on with amusement as inflatable footballs, bananas, sharks and even a crutch were all thrown around the away end before the match had kicked off. Fans were in good voice. We were here for a good day out and if Ipswich could win, that'd be the icing on a very satisfying cake. My brother didn't feel optimistic. He informed me before the match that he'd dreamt we'd lost 8-3. Given some of our performances since this fixture, I imagine we'd all quite like to see that much goal action. Rather like the fixture at Portman Road, two stubborn defences were set to clash horns. However, unlike the fixture at Portman Road, it was less of an even affair. Ipswich, in a typical McCarthy away performance, played determinedly, offering Watford nothing and allowed them the grand total of no shots on target. It was a decent Town performance. The defence had stood firm and the midfield had coped with the League leaders admirably. All that was missing was a goal. There had been shots, most of them long range and most of them sailing harmlessly past Gomes' posts. Given form, league position and McCarthy, it would've been a decent point. Then, in the 86th minute, loanee Richard Chaplow was thrown into the mix. Full-time edged closer. Town fans continued to chant and bat inflatable footballs around. Watford fans were getting frustrated. Four minutes were added on. Watford were in the Ipswich half but not in possession. Tyrone Mings headed the ball up. Jay Tabb got on the end of it and hooked the ball up field. The break was on. Freddie Sears, assisted by an awkward bounce between two Watford defenders, managed to get the ball and run towards the goal.

Meanwhile, Richard Chaplow was running through the middle. Sears, with a Watford player ahead of him, passed the ball across to an unmarked Chaplow. I can imagine how Watford fans felt when the ball hit the back of the net. Watching your side concede a last minute winner is one of the most painful experiences in football. For us in that away end, though, it was utter pandemonium. Inflatables went everywhere, people went everywhere (including onto the pitch). When a winner like that goes in, you end up six seats and two rows away from where you started. You attempt to high five or hug anyone within distance, you cheer until your voice is gone. The players, including the subs bench, head straight towards the fans. We'd already experienced the Noel Hunt winner at Charlton, where someone in front of us at The Valley celebrated so much he dislocated his shoulder. This Watford victory was different. The Charlton performance hadn't exactly been brilliant but here, at Vicarage Road, Town had been superb. It wasn't a daylight robbery but a deserved winner for a side who had managed to match, if not outplay, a league topping side.

What made it all the more special, though, was that I experienced it with my brother. We've always been close. I've always been the one he messages when he's after a sporting opinion, some analysis or calling Michael Vaughan a few choice words. I love away days, I love meeting up with my friends and going to the pub (despite not actually being a drinker), being able to discuss Ipswich Town with people who understand the passion. They are people you mainly see during the football season, who look after you from the station to the ground before going through the spectrum of emotions a football match brings. Then, when the day is over, you head off in your separate directions knowing that, no matter what the result or how bad the performance, you'll see each other again soon. And while those days are brilliant and hold many memories, away days with my brother are special. Football has always been a common bond between the two of us and has, as we've got older, brought us closer together. Because that's what football does: it brings people together. It's a sport with a fantastic sense of unity and it's something that is very difficult to explain to someone who doesn't "get" that. Some don't understand how twenty-two men kicking a ball around can rouse such feeling in people. But football isn't just about what happens on the pitch. Ipswich Town are, famously, a family club, so to share experiences like that last minute winner with someone incredibly close and important to you is, without a doubt, something that football is all about.

Hannah Sibley

Watford 0 Ipswich Town 1
Championship 2014/15
Attendance: 19,038
Referee: Andy D'Urso

WATFORD

Manager::   Slavisa Jokanovic

Team: Heurelho Gomes, Marco Motta, Craig
Cathcart, Joel Ekstrand, Tommy Hoban, Miguel Layun, Ben
Watson, Daniel Tozser, Adlène Guedioura, Odion Ighalo, Troy
Deeney. (Subs: Gabriele Angella, Matej Vydra, Ikechi Anya)

IPSWICH TOWN

Manager: Mick McCarthy

Team: Bartosz Bialkowski, Luke Chambers,
Tommy Smith, Christophe Berra, Tyrone Mings, Kévin Bru,
Cole Skuse, Jay Tabb, Chris Wood, Luke Varney, Daryl Murphy
(Subs: Paul Anderson, Richard Chaplow, Freddie Sears)

Goals: Chaplow (85)

TWELVE

Sheffield United 1 Ipswich Town 1
Saturday, 10 May 1997
Bramall Lane

Play-offs. Two words that few Ipswich Town fans can ever hear without recalling a whole host of memories. A few of them are even good ones: Wembley 2000, the Bolton semi-final, Tommy Smith running the length of Carrow Road to celebrate in front of two thousand ecstatic Town fans.

The best sport generally depends on two factors: competitive matches and scarcity value. Despite the best efforts of the richest clubs, disparities in the former can still be overcome which is what makes giant-killings so compelling, or hilarious depending on one's point of view. The latter though - the first Test of the Summer, the opening match of the World Cup Finals, the Summer Olympics - provides that real sense of expectation and excitement that fans really look forward to, even for those of us who are probably old enough to know better. This point is generally missed by TV schedulers but definitely understood by fans mid-way through a particularly rubbish season.

There is another factor though, one not always present but when it is, fans certainly know about it: sporting grudges.

Ipswich fans of a certain age have a clear lack of affection for Dean Saunders and Bob Hamer. Those a generation older probably can't hear the name Clive Thomas without falling into a paroxysm of swearing. For those who experienced these injustices, there is nothing irrational about this - well no more so than in watching football in the first place.

Put play-offs and the creation of a grudge together and we have Ipswich versus Sheffield United in 1997. A tie that created something of a rivalry, although only really on our part.

But first some context: relegation in 1994/95, one of the most abject seasons in the club's history, totally outclassed and heading for the drop from early in the season despite somehow managing to beat three of that season's top five.

The appointment of George Burley mid-way through that season did mark the beginning of an improvement, even if the signs were well hidden for a while. Ian Marshall's goal at Highbury, the first in 675 minutes spread over nearly two months was celebrated with great enthusiasm even though Arsenal led 4-0 at the time. Off the pitch things were changing too, David Sheepshanks took over as Chairman, freshening up a moribund board with talk of five-year plans and new toilets at Portman Road.

Any fears of Ipswich suffering a second successive relegation were quickly dispelled as a side which had scored only thirty-six goals became the highest scorers in the country with the addition only of Gus Uhlenbeek and, later in the season, Tony Mowbray. Those seventy-nine league goals however were not quite enough to make the play-offs and Town finished seventh by two points and the width of a post.

As importantly for me personally, I started university in 1995, and it was a lot more fun being able to check the football scores and see Ipswich winning than it might have been the previous year, one's football team very much a badge of identity at that age (well, OK any age but I would like to think I'm a bit more rounded twenty-plus years on). This despite being in the middle of an eighteen month spell of managing not to see a victory; the last match before going away a shambolic 5-1 home defeat to Charlton, with ended with striker Neil Gregory in goal, evidence that the previous season's defensive weakness had yet to be eradicated.

Despite all that, Town fans could allow themselves to be optimistic for the new season for the first time in a few years. The growing positivity reinforced for many fans by a very enjoyable Euro 1996 where the home team had performed well, only missing a place in the final by the centimeters Paul Gascoigne just couldn't quite manage to stretch and a penalty shoot-out defeat.

Ipswich started that season away at newly relegated Manchester City in a Friday night fixture most notable for Uhlenbeek's dyed blonde hair. The goals returned the following week as Reading were beaten 5-2. That match included a first Ipswich goal for Mauricio Taricco. The Argentine full-back, initially seen as a makeweight when signed with Adrian Paz the previous season, had slowly forced his way into Burley's side, impressing fans with his skill and tenacity.

And then Ipswich sold Ian Marshall. After scoring twenty-five goals across his first two seasons at the club, a feat notable considering the scarcity of goals from that side, Marshall and strike partner Alex Mathie had both scored nineteen immediately after relegation and fans were hoping for more of the same. A pressing overdraft intervened however and Marshall headed for Leicester where notable goal scoring feats including one at the Estadio Vicente Calderón awaited him.

Selling the club's most important striker in August does not tend to be a harbinger of a successful season but things got worse for Ipswich when Alex Mathie injured a shoulder scoring the equalizer in a 3-3 draw at Oldham. Despite a few more appearances - and nine goals by late October - a shoulder operation ended his season.

The loss of both Marshall and Mathie left the club with only a young James Scowcroft and Neil Gregory as the only strikers with any first team experience and not a great deal of that. With money tight, Burley supplemented the squad with loanees with mixed results: I listened to one home defeat to Tranmere on local Merseyside radio and at the mention of Gerry Creaney I thought that I hadn't known that he was playing for them, only to slowly realise that he wasn't playing for Tranmere.

League form that Autumn was decidedly mixed. September was generally good despite a home defeat to Huddersfield. It included a comeback from a goal down to beat Sheffield United 3-1 at Bramall Lane, a match also notable for the sending off of Michel Vonk, the second season in succession that the home team had a had a player sent off in that fixture and another game against Charlton the weekend I returned to university for my second year. This time we won 2-1, thanks to an excellently placed free kick from Sedgley and a goal from Mathie.

Results then tailed off in October and November, at one stage Town going six matches without a win before a Paul Mason goal at QPR changed that. Even so, by late-November the team had gone two months without a home league win until two wins in a week against Swindon and Port Vale improved the mood at Portman Road a bit and a late away win at league leaders Bolton Wanderers was impressive.

In contrast to the league form, a good run in the League Cup (this was the 1990s...) had seen Town to the quarter finals and by the end of the year more young players emerged with Richard Naylor scoring his first goals for the club and Kieron Dyer making his debut in a Boxing Day win over Crystal Palace. In addition the club's finances were stretched enough to sign Jason Cundy from Spurs after an impressive loan spell.

Town began to steadily climb the table in the new year - another impressive away victory at a Barnsley side heading for promotion was followed by a run of four successive home victories interspersed with away draws. In one of them, away to Port Vale, Paul Mason scored one of the great forgotten Town goals after running from his own half, checking back and curling the ball into the top corner. Mason made something of a habit of the spectacular that season, several impressive volleys featuring amongst his fifteen goals.

That successful run was halted by a home defeat to Bolton also by this time clearly heading for promotion, but three days later a Neil Gregory hat-trick (essentially the same goal three times in the first half) beat Sheffield United. Easter, however, saw successive away defeats and the play-off challenge appeared to be in the balance.

Ipswich recovered well and promptly won five matches in a row, scoring twelve times without conceding a goal, even more improbably this was achieved with a defence including Tony Vaughan and Chris Swailes. It did though feature Steve Sedgley, playing the best football of his Town career sat between the two stoppers and breaking forward into midfield; he was more like a proper *libero* than the plodding midfielder seen for much of his first two seasons at Portman Road.

The highlight of this spell was a Friday night victory over Norwich in the East Anglian Derby. Mauricio Taricco ran onto Sedgley's glorious pass to open the scoring past Andy Marshall before another volley from Paul Mason made it 2-0 but really it could have been several more.

The season finished with a 1-1 draw at home to Birmingham, Town's goal scored by Niklas Gudmundsson another loanee brought in by Burley to help replace Marshall and Mathie. Ipswich finished fourth and would play Sheffield United in a two-legged semi final.

Back in May 1997, Ipswich fans memories of play-offs were rather more benign than they are today although the club had featured in the inaugural play-offs at the end of the 1986/87 season, losing 2-1 to Charlton over two legs. In my naïvety, I confidently expected the better team from the season just gone to prevail, failing to recognize that play-offs aren't really play-offs without outrageous shifts in fortune and sudden drama.

At it was, I was pre-occupied not only with the biggest match for several seasons but also my impending second year exams. Apparently spending time on the internet, looking for any information or comment about a big match isn't particularly conducive to revision: so it was a good thing that the only place I could access the internet in those days was the university library.

By the time of the Friday night before the game, I think I was wittering on about the next day's match to anyone who would listen, which I'm sure was a fairly limited number of people by the end of the night.

The following morning I set off for Sheffield with an ever-rising sense of expectation. Not that I was the only one. 5,500 Ipswich fans made the journey to Sheffield filling both tiers of the away end. Even heavy rain upon arrival and a very limited choice of suitable-looking pubs around Bramall Lane did little to dampen the mood.

Despite all the early enthusiasm, the game did not get off to a good start, Jan Aage-Fjortoft - a player who might have left English football three seasons earlier but for managing to score for Swindon against us in an FA Cup tie - was allowed too much space and beat Richard Wright rather easily at his near post.

The support of the Ipswich fans didn't waver though: 1-0 down, soaked through and still singing non-stop, it was fun and one of the best atmospheres I can remember. Despite a couple of presentable chances for the home side there were no further goals in the first half and Ipswich had a chance to regroup.

Burley brought on Gudmundsson for Neil Gregory and, as the sun came out, Ipswich played their way back into the match. Eventually, Mick Stockwell ran onto a through ball to take the ball past the goalkeeper and thump home a very well-deserved equaliser. At the time, we were making so much noise anyway that I didn't quite know how to celebrate. I jumped round 360 degrees for some odd reason. I doubt anyone actually noticed given the general state of the reaction around me.

The match finished 1-1 and, on the back of Ipswich's very good home form, a win seemed the most likely outcome of the home leg four days afterwards. Unfortunately that was the day of my last exam and there was no feasible way of making it back to Ipswich in time for the match. That disappointment was assuaged by the thought of a trip to Wembley for the final.

Things didn't go to plan however, Vaughan was easily beaten by Petr Katchuro who gave the away side an early league but Scowcroft, bleeding from an earlier clash of heads, equalized before half-time heading home a ball in from Taricco.

In the second half Niklas Gudmundsson put Town ahead for the first time in the tie with only seventeen minutes to go. Another defensive lapse however took the match into extra time. With almost the last kick of the match Sedgley curled a free kick against the post at the North Stand end with the goalkeeper well beaten. The tie finished 3-3 but Sheffield United prevailed on the away goals rule. The match ended with the unpleasant Fjortoft goading Taricco, blaming him for the sending off of yet another Sheffield United player.

On the face of it then, perhaps not a match that should stand out as a favourite but its significance still resonates two decades on. For me, and many other Town fans, it marked a first real experience of the drama of the play-offs, that constant half-excited, half-fearful distillation of an entire season into a couple of matches. Such a painful way to lose but a glorious way to win.

In the fullness of time, Town gained ample revenge both for play-off failure and the manner of the defeat to Sheffield United, victory at Wembley in 2000 was so much better and so much more deserved for the three years of play-off failure and disappointment that preceded it. The same sense of satisfaction, albeit on a lesser scale, also met the annual victory over Sheffield United during the Joe Royle years.

It also marked an important step in the transition from the dire relegation side of 1994/95, to an entertaining and competitive one, a side whose fans could realistically expect to see it challenging for promotion. Not only that, but it was a team that had overcome adversity, firstly with the loss of both of the previous seasons's top scorers but also the absence of Jason Cundy who missed the end of the season to have treatment for testicular cancer.

In many ways though, the team that played in this semi-final had reached its end, a step on the way to the better, more entertaining side that would eventually win promotion in 2000. Sedgley left for Wolves, although that worked out an excellent deal with Mark Venus and moving to Ipswich in addition to a transfer fee, Vaughan for Manchester City and Uhlenbeek to Fulham.

The following season saw the return of Cundy and Mathie, the emergence of Bobby Petta and the continued development of Scowcroft, Dyer and Naylor together with the signings of Matt Holland and David Johnson. The latter, in November provided the goals to kickstart a technically better side a long way up the league - before losing in the play-offs again.

The player who emerged from that Sheffield United tie with the greatest reputation amongst Ipswich fans however was Mauricio Taricco. The Argentinian had established himself as an important part of Burley's side over the preceding two seasons but it was the reaction to losing the tie that truly endeared him to fans: "They don't like me, I don't like them." True cult heroes don't turn up all that regularly but one did here and that is the final reason that makes this tie so memorable.

Stephen Moore

Sheffield United 1 Ipswich Town 1
Division One Play-off Semi-final, 1996/97
Attendance: 22,312
Referee: Roy Pearson

SHEFFIELD UNITED

Manager: Howard Kendall

Team: Alan Kelly, Mitch Ward, Roger Nilsen, Don Hutchison, Carl Tiler, David Holdsworth, David White, Nick Henry, Jan Åge Fjørtoft, Petr Katchouro, Dane Whitehouse (Subs: Gareth Taylor, Chris Short)

Goals: Fjørtoft (41)

IPSWICH TOWN

Manager: George Burley

Team: Richard Wright, Mick Stockwell, Mauricio Taricco, Steve Sedgley, Chris Swailes, Geraint Williams, Gus Uhlenbeek, Tony Vaughan, Neil Gregory, James Scowcroft, Kieron Dyer (Subs: Niklas Gudmundsson)

Goals: Stockwell (78)

THIRTEEN

Torpedo Moscow 1 Ipswich Town 2
Thursday, 27 September 2001
Luzhniki Stadium

Awkward. This is getting very awkward.

In that way that men with a low centre of gravity tend to have, Marcus Stewart kind of toddles on his way to the penalty spot. I watch through my fingers as he short-arses up to strike the ball.

It all goes wrong.

An inebriated man bearhugs me. Someone's mum in the row behind loses her bobble hat. She reaches over me to retrieve it and kisses one of my ears as two middle aged blokes grab at me for a beery group po-go.

Oh God. They think I'm one of them. I'm trapped.

I can hardly blame them though. I'm amongst the travelling Ipswich Town supporters in Torpedo Moscow's brutalist Luzhniki stadium. The Super Blues have just gone 2-0 up in the return match of a September 2001 UEFA Cup tie, putting them through to the next round.

This may not be the best time to let slip that I am in fact a season ticket holder in the Barclay at Norwich City along for the ride with my Ipswich Town supporting girlfriend. She's on my left with a slightly scary beatific expression on her face as if some kind of divine revelation has manifested itself in the centre circle.

For some reason, Talking Heads come to mind. - *My God! What have I done? This is not my beautiful wife.* - But it's this bit that really nails it: - *And you may say to yourself, well... how did I get here?*

The story of how Emma and I met is like some kind of El Tractico take on *Romeo and Juliet*. Back in 1999, Norwich and Ipswich fans arranged a football match before the following day's derby at Carrow Road. I ran the line, Emma was there with her Ipswich supporting friends.

Like Tony and Maria in *West Side Story* our eyes met and we found love across the great divide (except none of Emma's friends got their "father's gun" and tried to shoot me.) So it all started with a touching display of cross border unity - a truce which held for as long as Norwich and Ipswich were generally as crap as each other. Then Norwich drifted down into Championship mediocrity as Ipswich got good, finished fifth in the Premiership and qualified for Europe.

When the UEFA Cup draw sent Ipswich to Moscow, I did the calculations. Obviously it would be great to go to Moscow before neo-liberalism completely erased all trace of the previous regime. Who wouldn't want to get their picture taken next to the city's stirring constructivist remnants of the failed workers' state? At the very least, it'd make a nice change from Hemsby.

To get more time in Russia, we didn't travel with the club. That meant a greatly reduced chance of contact with unknown Town fans who might rumble me by asking for my views on Glenn Pennyfather and whether Adrian Paz's best position was winger or striker. (Google tells me it's not really either for the latter player.)

But most importantly, after a 1-1 home draw with Torpedo I really couldn't see Ipswich staying in the competition after the second leg. It would be my own personal act of yellow and green espionage to be recounted down the pub in Norwich - maybe with a few duty-free vodka chasers after closing time.

I've often suspected I may not be a terribly good loser but when the second goal went in I discovered a new talent for sulking at 2-0 up. I wrestled myself free of the celebrations and marched up the aisle, scuttling under the forest of high-fives stretching arcing over the steps. Finally, I reached the line of smoking, rather underemployed Russian police at the top of the stand.

To pass the time, I thought it'd be good to try out some of my very limited Russian while I was there. I cope fine with a bit of chat about the weather. Trading my B&H for the local rough-as-arseholes Belomor fags, we sagely compare smokes. The international language of football - mainly nodding along to people saying "Manchester United" and "Paul Gascoigne" and Subbuteo-miming great World Cup goals - takes me a bit closer to full-time. But things get more difficult after that.

I discovered there's very little in the Berlitz *Russian for Travellers* phrasebook which helps explain to a group of Russian nineteen-year-olds with machine guns that even though you are with this group of "hooligans," you actually want the Moscow team to win. It's even trickier to get it across that you are actually a supporter of the English team's fiercest rivals, that Norwich is a city in the east of england mainly famous for its mustard and has a market "on the huh."

"Hooligans" is a word I hear quite a lot in Moscow. It gets round which hotels the Ipswich fans are staying in and when we go to meet some of Emma's friends, the entrances are honour guarded by Russian fans in double denim waiting to see their English counterparts and swap football memorabilia. The Ipswich contingent aren't "fans" or "supporters" - all the talk is of Ipswich, Torpedo, Spartak, Dynamo and Lokomotiv Moscow "hooligans." Whether that's a translation thing or something else, I never found out.

However, we did discover a few visitor-only services offered by the local police in and around Red Square. No doubt keen to help tourists frustrated by the queues to get into Lenin's Mausoleum, we were offered the opportunity of a special visit. For fifty dollars, we could get "really close" to the embalmed leader of the revolution in the Kremlin after hours.

Less helpfully, several Ipswich fans found themselves subjected to a special on-the-spot fine of ten dollars for "smoking in Red Square." Apparently, it was five dollars for walking on the cracks in the pavement too.

It had been over decade since Russia swapped Soviet paranoid autocracy for something which has turned out to be scarily similar but just run in the interests of the international super rich instead. The change certainly didn't seem to have benefited the scores of dead-eyed older people on every

Moscow street - forced to sell their paltry possessions to supplement their increasingly worthless state pensions.

However, the shadow of the former USSR still cast itself into corners of the city. The complex of hotels we stayed in hadn't yet got into that cringey, friendly corporation mode. For better listing inventory style, the hotels were still named Alpha, Beta, Gamma and so forth. They also seemed to cling to old traditions of Soviet customer service which included what must surely count as the world's most disgusting breakfast buffet.

A typical menu comprised some unidentifiable sweaty meat items with the slight odour of light industrial areas. There was something a bit like fish which looked like it had been trawled in radioactive waters using a rusty net and then given the bumps.

Blinis - which are a real treat in the UK - were submerged in what must have been surplus tractor transmission oil. And of course there were pickled things - lots of them. All grey-green in some kind of after birth-like mucous.

I really didn't enjoy the game against Torpedo and I don't support Ipswich so you might be wondering what this tale is doing in a book about favourite Ipswich matches. However as it's still my one and only experience of going in with the Ipswich fans, I suppose it counts by default.

I learnt a lot of things from my visit to Moscow - including how Russians think it's impolite to put your bag on the ground and will insist you put it on an a chair instead, But the biggest thing I learnt was not to tempt fate by going in with the Ipswich fans. I've been with Emma to a few other Ipswich away games since the Torpedo match but now I make sure to sit with the home support.

Adam Green

Torpedo Moscow 1 Ipswich Town 2
UEFA Cup, First Round, Second Leg, 2001/2
Attendance: c.10,500
Referee: Pascal Garibian

TORPEDO MOSCOW

Manager: Vitali Shevchenko

Team: Roman Berezovsky, Andrei Malai, Ediki
Sadjaia, Nikola Jolovich, Viacheslav Daev, Aliaksandr
Lukhvich, Alexande Shirko, Vladimir Leonchenko, Dmitry
Vyazmikin, Sergiy Kormyltsev, Konstantin Zyranyov (Subs:
Andrei Gashkin, Jovica Lakic, Igor Semshov)

Goals: Vyazmikin (65)

IPSWICH TOWN

Manager: George Burley

Team: Matteo Sereni, Chris Makin, Hermann
Hreidarsson, John McGreal, Mark Venus, Jamie Clapham,
Finidi George, Matt Holland, Jim Magilton, Alun Armstrong,
Marcus Stewart (Subs: Tommy Miller, Jermaine Wright,
Richard Naylor)

Goals: George (46)
             Stewart (54 pen.)

Contributors

Grant Bage saw his first Ipswich game in 1967 and has been going ever since. Although he has written several books for children, and for adult audiences, his regular articles in the *Turnstile Blues* fanzine are much more fun: or at least ... they are for the writer!

Gavin Barber has been watching Ipswich Town since 1983. He's a former editor of Ipswich fanzines *Blue* and *Those Were The Days*, and now writes for *Turnstile Blues*, as well as making occasional contributions to *When Saturday Comes*. His favourite ever Ipswich players are Jason Dozzell, Mauricio Taricco, and Mick Stockwell, and he is proud that the only people ever to block him on Twitter are Andrew Neil and Michael Chopra.

Emma Corlett was brought up on a weekly diet of Ipswich Town and Colchester United during the 1980s. She stuck with Ipswich Town yet has lived in Norwich, where she trained as a mental health nurse, since 1996.

Rob Freeman was born in the West Midlands, but has been an Ipswich Town fan ever since his father first took him to Portman Road during the John Duncan Days. As if that wasn't masochistic in itself, Rob now lives and works in Norwich.

Susan Gardiner has been a season ticket holder at Portman Road since 2001. She has written about Town and other things for various printed and online publications, the highpoint of which was writing about Sir Bobby Robson for the official 2016 UEFA Cup Final programme. Her first book, *Ipswich Town: A History* was published in 2013 and her most recent - a biography of the England international, Frank Soo - is currently with the censors in China.

Adam Green is a season ticket holder in the Barclay Stand at Carrow Road who, for reasons he explains, stood with Ipswich Town fans in Moscow in September 2001,

Stuart Hellingsworth works in local government, is an active trade unionist and is the eastern region chair of Rethink Mental Illness. He also delights in suffering through supporting Ipswich Town while living in Norfolk.

Steve Moore is a long-standing Town fan still retaining a sense of optimism about ITFC. Otherwise to be found watching cricket or somewhere in the mountains.

Chris Rand watched his first Ipswich Town match in 1968, in the days when small boys were lifted over to sit on the grass in front of the advertising hoardings. He never looked back.

Beginning her 40th season as an Ipswich fan, **Sarah Rogers** is a season ticket holder in the Co-op stand. She intersperses attendance at Portman Road with a day job in the cultural sector.

Alasdair Ross's claim to fame is that Laurie Sivell, Ipswich Town & Germany (*Escape To Victory*) goalkeeper used to lodge with his parents.

Seán Salter: "My Dad took me to my first game forty years ago and I immediately fell in love with Town. I feasted on the glories of Robson, Lyall and Burley. I've now passed the baton on to my two children. I apologise to them both for the Paul Jewell era."

Hannah Sibley is a season ticket holder in the lower tier of the Sir Bobby Robson Stand. She has been an Ipswich fan for seventeen years so can just about remember life outside the Championship.

Lightning Source UK Ltd.
Milton Keynes UK
UKOW01f1034220917
309680UK00009B/292/P